CHARIS PUBLISHING, LLC
P.O. Box 12
Chatham, Virginia 24531

First originally published by Charis Publishing 2024

ISBN 979-8-218-40623-3 (Hardcover)
ISBN 979-8-218-40644-8 (Digital)

For author speaking appearances, please
contact Sonya Womack-Miranda via
email:
charisancestryconnections@gmail.com
For the latest book signings and events:
Please visit the website:
www.unnamedsarahmiller.com

Printed in the United States of America

DEDICATION

This book is dedicated to the family historians who generously shared my history. All of them are descendants of former slaves and later sharecroppers and or farmers.

1. Alberta Miller Womack (cousin) – born in rural Pittsylvania County, Virginia; migrated to New York City. (Miller Family Historian)
2. Linda Stephens (cousin) – born in Halifax County, Virginia; migrated to the greater Washington DC area. (Luck Family Historian)
3. Anglean Miller (grandmother) – born in Pittsylvania County, Virginia; lived there until her passing. (Miller Family Historian)
4. Douglas Womack (cousin) – born in Halifax County, Virginia; migrated to Boston, Massachusetts. (Womack Family Historian)
5. Martha Ann Womack Ragsdale (paternal aunt) – born in Halifax County, Virginia; lived there until her passing. (Luck, Womack Family Historian)
6. Robert Miller (cousin) – born in Pittsylvania County, Virginia; migrated to Prince George's County, Maryland. (Luck Family Historian)
7. Reverand Charlie M. Miller (maternal grandfather) – born in rural Pittsylvania County, Virginia; lived there until his passing. (Miller Family Historian)
8. Joan Miller Womack (mother) – born in Pittsylvania County, Virginia. (Maternal, Paternal Miller Family Historian)

TRIBUTE

In a world teeming with wonders and extraordinary moments, one remarkable force has shaped my existence with boundless love and unwavering fortitude. This tribute is a heartfelt homage to the guiding light of my life, my cherished mother, Joan Miller Womack. Your presence has filled my life with an abundance of strength and affection, weaving resilience and compassion into the very fabric of my being. Your unwavering support has been my anchor through life's storms, your embrace a haven of comfort and solace. With each beat of my heart, I carry the essence of your boundless love, a beacon illuminating my path through life's challenges. This dedication is more than mere words; it is a testament to the enduring influence of a mother's love—a flame that burns eternally within my soul. I dedicate this book to you, Ma.

CONTENTS

FOREWORD

History is Knowing Who You Are

It is of utmost importance that we, as a community, grasp a deep understanding of our origins and heritage. In an era when there is a concerted effort to suppress our African American history, our vigilance to explore and learn from our past becomes paramount. By doing so, we can gain a profound appreciation for the challenges our ancestors confronted. This act of self-education not only inspires love and compassion for those who have paved the way before us but also nurtures the courage within us to continue to move forward.

Ancestry serves as the vital link between family and society. The journeys undertaken by our ancestors and the knowledge of our lineage can profoundly influence both personal and collective identities. It allows us to mentally retrace their paths and develop a deep gratitude for our own lives. Our ancestors lived, thrived, loved, and endured hardships long before our time, and their experiences continue to resonate in our lives today. Without them, we wouldn't be here, and it is imperative that we acknowledge their significance.

The events chronicled in this book transpired in the rural landscapes of Pittsylvania County, Virginia, during an era of slavery, that inhumane practice of one individual owning another, legally, deeming them as property or chattel and stripping them of all rights. It is evident that the institution of slavery dictated a certain measure of prosperity for some while inflicting tragic, cruel, and harsh living conditions upon others.

This narrative follows the search of a young woman named Sarah Miller and her family. Sarah Miller's parents were among the enslaved, and she was one of eight children in a household of twelve, residing in a small cabin on the Sharswood Plantation. Most stories of slavery unveil the heart-wrenching accounts of childhood and adult abuse, and numerous publications highlight the myriad of hardships endured throughout a slave's life. Even though Sarah Miller was born three years after the formal end of slavery, its brutal legacies and deep-seated prejudices endured. Sarah's life was marked by hardship, and this narrative delves into the context of her parents being among the "Un-Named."

To explore Sarah Miller's lineage and her experiences on the plantation, we examined the concept of the "Un-Named" as our guiding light through the myriad of questions we encountered while penning this story. In the pages that follow, we shall reveal the triumphant tale of how Sarah's forebears survived the harrowing voyage known today as the Transatlantic Slave Trade or the Middle Passage, ultimately witnessing their descendants reclaim their historical legacy.

Zoe Charis Miranda, age 19
Sarah Miller's third great-granddaughter

PREFACE

"If they had no names, how did you find them?" This was the probing question posed to me by Leslie Stahl during an interview while recording the "Sharswood" story for *60 Minutes*. It was a question that left me momentarily speechless, caught off guard by the stark reality that my ancestors had indeed been among the "Un-Named." My face flushed, and my tongue felt tied in knots as I struggled to respond. I had never truly contemplated the implications of this fact until that very moment. I had the answers, I had found them all, but on that day, in that 60 Minutes interview, I found myself unable to articulate how.

Imagine the challenge of tracing ancestors who were once enslaved, individuals who weren't even recognized as human beings. They endured the perilous Transatlantic Ocean voyage on ships, stripped of their names, identities, tribal affiliations, home countries, and languages of origin. There were no tickets or ship manifestos recording their passage or journey.

Uncovering the name of an enslaved ancestor is a difficult task for African Americans. When I embarked on this journey to unveil my lineage, many of the resources available today were not at my disposal. Nevertheless, I remained captivated and resolute in my mission to identify those I came to know as the "Un-Named." I will now narrate the story of how I meticulously reconstructed my family history and linked numerous enslaved individuals who had previously existed in obscurity on the Sharswood plantation.

Through my research and discovery, I unearthed a hidden past, one I could hardly believe. I traced the connection of my ancestors to their Caucasian slave owners. It was truly astonishing to unveil the extent to which my history had been veiled in mystery, with my ancestors' names deliberately hidden and omitted from historical documents. Yet, against all odds, I succeeded in forging a profound connection to each one of my ancestors. This raised a crucial question: why have some gone to such lengths to conceal our past, our lineage, our connection to our ancestral homeland, and our place in the tapestry of human existence? We were led to believe that no records of their names existed, that they were part of the vast Un-Named those who were not recorded by name prior to the 1870 census- and we lamented that their names were taken from us, sold away, and hidden from us.

But I found them.

A decade ago, my journey into the depths of my family's history commenced, prompted by the heartfelt encouragement of my mother, Joan Miller Womack. My mother and her father, Charlie M. Miller, both possessed a profound passion for Black history. Their shared desire was to unravel the enigma of their own roots and trace the origins of our family's heritage. My grandfather, a lifelong inhabitant of Pittsylvania County, Virginia, held a treasure trove of knowledge about the region, including its significant landmarks, influential figures, and the rich tapestry of places that defined Pittsylvania County.

For me, this endeavor was not just about belief; it was about establishing a profound connection to remarkable ancestors. This connection symbolized a sense of completeness and wholeness, where the missing pieces of the puzzle was found and rejoined. Yet, for people of African descent, this sentiment is often met with some degree of complexity. The history of being forcibly torn from their homeland, their heritage, and their families during the era of enslavement left an enduring void. How could one ever truly feel whole when such vital aspects of their identity had been cruelly severed?

At the heart of our family's history was Charlie M. Miller, a man whose wisdom transcended the boundaries of generations. With a twinkle in his eye and stories that danced on the winds of time, "Grandpa Dea," as we affectionately knew him, became the original Miller historian. His love for family and heritage was infectious, and he instilled in us a passion for uncovering the hidden treasures of our ancestry. Charlie was a walking encyclopedia of the Miller family's journey, and he reveled in sharing tales of courage, resilience, and triumph. He spoke of ancestors who had weathered the storms of slavery and segregation, emerging as pillars of strength in their communities. Through his words, he painted a vivid picture of their struggles and their unwavering commitment to family and freedom.

Beside Charlie stood Joan Miller Womack, a woman of profound faith and boundless love. She was a beacon of light in our lives, illuminating the path towards self-acceptance and the richness of our Black culture. Joan's gentle yet unwavering guidance encouraged our family to embrace our identity with pride, to understand that our roots ran deep, and our worth was immeasurable.

In the heart of this familial tapestry was my father William Womack Jr., who embodied the essence of identity and heritage. Fearless and unyielding in his beliefs, he imparted knowledge in me. I was his first-born daughter, Sonya Womack. He taught me that my voice mattered, and that my identity was a source of strength, and that standing up for what I believed in was my birthright. His spirit of resilience and unwavering determination became a legacy that now resides within me.

Charlie Miller, Joan Miller Womack, and William Womack Jr. left behind a profound legacy that transcended generations. Their collective efforts to preserve and share our family's history served as a testament to the enduring power of self-discovery, heritage, and the pursuit of truth. In their memory, I continued my quest, guided by their spirits, taking each step toward a deeper understanding of the intricate and diverse tapestry of my heritage.

In the embrace of this remarkable family, as a young Black girl growing up in rural Virginia, I found the courage to explore the depths of my identity, to celebrate the richness of my culture, and to stand unapologetically in my truth. I learned that history was not just a distant tale but a living, breathing legacy carried in the hearts and minds of those who came before me.

Though Charlie, William, and Joan did not live to witness my return to our motherland of Africa, their legacies were enduring beacons of inspiration for me to journey there. Their combined wisdom and passion for uncovering the past continued to fuel my determination to trace my lineage back to the distant shores of Africa and to Great Britain. In their absence, I carry their spirits with me, knowing that I walk the path they had paved with love, knowledge, and a thirst for truth.

INTRODUCTION

This narrative unveils the story of my family, the Millers of rural Pittsylvania County, Virginia. It delves into how I forged a connection between the African American Millers of Pittsylvania County, Virginia, to the **Sharswood Plantation**. My aspiration is to shed light on how, with the assistance of technology, it has become increasingly accessible for individuals to delve into their past and forge connections with their ancestors. The tracing of one's family lineage and heritage is made possible through the collection of valuable clues passed down through generations, often preserved by family elders.

This books sheds light on the extensive decade-long research, the invaluable insights gathered from conversations with family elders, and the connections that link the slaves, often referred to as the *"Un-Named,"* to the plantation owners. Within these pages lies an incredible story that directly intertwines my African American ancestors with their Caucasian slaveholders. The complete, untold story could not be encapsulated within a sin-gle 60 Minute segment. It was an arduous eleven-year journey that culminated in a remarkable one-hour feature on 60 minutes. Yet there is much more to delve into regarding the remaining links and connections to our African American heritage and how our story unfolded.

Within the pages of this book, I embark on a journey into a place that held a special place in the heart of my Miller grand-fa-ther, lovingly referred to as the "Miller Plantation." The history of the Miller plantation wasn't a hidden secret; it was an inseparable part of their daily lives. It was the place they knew they and their ancestors had descended from; a living legacy woven into the fabric of their existence. Indeed, among my family members, myself included, tales of the magnificent residence on Riceville Road, now known as "Sharswood," have been passed down through generations. Throughout the course of this narrative, I consistently employ the term "Miller Plantation" to affectionately speak of Sharswood, mirroring the way our ancestors referred to it.

Our Ancestors Journey to North American Plantations

Africans stand as one of the most spiritually resilient people on Earth. From the heart of Alkebulan, they embarked on treacherous journeys in hollow, hand-carved vessels, akin to sardines, crossing the unforgiving Transatlantic Ocean, even subsisting on meager sustenance. In the face of both human cruelty and the harsh forces of nature, they clung to their unwavering faith, an unbreakable bond with the Almighty. Their ancestors possessed hearts and minds forged from steel or something even more unyielding. Shackled aboard ships, their imaginations soared beyond confinement, their prayers coursing through every vessel in their bodies, regardless of circumstances. This unshakable spirituality enabled Black individuals to not only endure the horrors of slavery and the fracturing of their families but to emerge stronger. In the crucible of the Middle Passage, Africans drew upon their ancestral fortitude and faith, emerging with their minds and souls intact. Their survival stands as a testament to their indomitable spirit.

I believe it's crucial to acknowledge and understand the historical struggles that African Americans have faced throughout their journey across the Transatlantic into the United States. From enduring slavery to grappling with the challenges of Jim Crow laws and segregation, African Americans have demonstrated incredible resilience and strength. Even after the formal end of slavery, we continued to face significant obstacles in our pursuit of equality, freedom, and the preservation of our heritage.

The legacy of slavery and the trauma it caused didn't disappear overnight. Many formerly enslaved people and their descendants confronted poverty, discrimination, and violence in the post-Civil War era. Even today we must navigate a society that can be hostile to our aspirations and rights. Despite these challenges, we have worked tirelessly to maintain our history, heritage, and family structures. Our African American, communities have a rich cultural heritage that we've preserved and celebrated through various means, such as music, literature, art, and oral traditions. But in my research and speaking to African Americans many struggle to trace their lineage beyond grandmothers.

Maya Angelou said, "The more you know of your history, the more liberated you are." Knowledge of one's history imbues a profound sense of greatness. Conversely, a lack of such knowledge can leave one feeling incomplete, as if nothing more than an unfinished human being. This absence of historical identity formed the basis for the removal of names, the erasure of history, and the systematic division of families. I often wonder whether the removing of ancestral names, language, and culture served as tools of control during this dark period we called slavery.

Recording Oral History

Inexplicably, my grandfather dedicated himself to preserving the legacy of our ancestors. He meticulously documented their names, identities, and even their images. Additionally, he regaled us with oral accounts of the landmarks and stories that had shaped his life in the rural corners of Pittsylvania County, Virginia. These narratives, handed down through generations, became the foundation of a profound *awakening* within me—a journey that would unravel the tapestry of my identity and trace my lineage back through time. Our family shared an unwavering commitment to the preservation of our ancestral history. As I delved deeper into the treasure trove of our heritage, I felt a profound calling to consistently record and safeguard this journey. My ultimate aim? To share this remarkable journey with you.

Over the course of my journey, I've had the privilege of engaging with various branches of the Miller and Womack families, collecting the rich oral history they've shared. I believe it to be a blessing to bear the title of Miller and Womack family historian, entrusted with the responsibility of recording, preserving, and chronicling the story of my family for generations yet to come. My intent and hope in sharing these stories is to inspire others to embark on their own quests to explore their past and uncover their ancestral roots. I hope to plant the seed that causes others to want to know themselves, their ancestors, and their story.

CHAPTER
ONE
The Tree of Life

A question demands an answer. But the answers to some questions we may never know, as attempting to respond can send you on a lifelong journey, perhaps a journey of no return or perhaps toward the path that changes everything.

This story begins on a beautiful Sunday near the end of summer, a day where you just feel alive, as if the possibilities are endless. I was in the kitchen when my phone rang, startling me from vague thoughts of how to spend my lazy afternoon. I answered, not realizing that this phone call would alter my life, and that I would begin a journey to discover parts of myself I didn't realize were missing. I can remember the details like it was yesterday. Little did I know that a simple phone call could alter one's life as much as it did mine on September 10, 2017. This call would send me on a lifelong errand, a journey of unearthing history, family, and finding self.

"Sonya," the person replied in a weary and tired voice, and I recognized Joan Miller Womack, my mother, the most influential person in my life. "Sonya, do you promise to continue to find our tree of life?" My mother and I had been on a journey together, uncovering our hidden "no named" ancestors, and she referred to our search as "connecting to the tree of life." She asked me this question often, but I did not understand why she was asking it out of the blue on this day. But in less than twenty-four hours, I would realize I would have to continue this journey of self-discovery alone.

Joan may have been the child of a sharecropper, but trust me when I say that she was a force to be reckoned with. She was an avid reader and lover of books. Her father, Charlie Miller, was well-versed in Black history and had passed on his experiences and knowledge to Joan. Like a butterfly, Joan had learned to change shape and form where and when necessary and live life without boundaries. She had taught me how to release my mind to see and visit faraway places without being physically present. From her, I learned that the name of a thing determines its being; if you do not give a being a name, you rob it of its sting. And so, Joan Miller Womack intentionally had no name for what many call "limits."

I had stood by my mother's hospital bed a few years earlier at the University of Virginia for an emergency procedure. There, the fear of death laying its icy hands on the woman I so adored had put me into a state of emptiness and despair. As I held Zoe, my four-year-old daughter, my hands were in Ma's. The doctors had told me to prepare her last will as she slipped into our ancestral realm. With our hands locked together, I knelt by her bedside and prayed to God earnestly not to take her away.

I felt a tremendous energy in the room, and at that moment, her eyes opened. With some difficulty, she called for her granddaughter and kissed Zoe's cheek. I told her what the doctors had said, that she was likely to pass away soon, and in a very Joan Miller Womack fashion, she chuckled loudly and said, "What do they know? Are they God?" and I could only laugh at my mother as that was the typical Joan response.

As I sat by Ma's bedside, she told me about her life and how fulfilling it had been. She told me how she moved from one farm to another as a child with her father, Charlie, a sharecropper, and Baptist minister. She told me that although this experience was not easy, it was rich in what mattered, as they learned the values of family and the need to stick together. She told me how, in later years, she had met a strong and confident Black man who was never afraid to speak his mind. How the two of them were so much alike and how this mystery man came to sweep her off her feet through his craftiness with words and his love for music.

Her voice filled with love as she told me about tying the knot with William Womack Jr., my father. Ma told me of her dream of looking out her kitchen window and seeing her grandchildren play in a flower garden. She had made this dream a reality through the purchase of a three-bedroom rancher in Ringgold, Virginia, where she'd planted carefully selected flowers to develop one of the most beautiful gardens in Mount Zion Circle. Ma told me she derived great joy from watching her three grand-daughters (Nyla, Zoe, and Skylar) play in the back yard of a home that was *hers*. After all, as the daughter of a sharecropper and only three generations removed from slavery, it was an honor to own her dream house, see her daughters graduate from college, and see her grandchildren play in her fairytale garden. As she lay in that hospital bed, I could feel that the only thing left for her joy to be complete was to visit the motherland – Africa.

In a flash, I recalled something that happened when I was twelve years old. Ma and I had been going through a National Geographic magazine when she pointed to a group of people from Senegal. She then said something to me that would shake the very core of my existence. "Sonya, do you see these people? This is who we are. We are not from this country. They brought us here." As my eyes grew wide, she gripped my hand and said, "We are from Africa!"

Seated by Ma's side in the hospital, I had a spark of inspiration, something I could bargain with, something that would help her to fight. I leaned forward and told her we would plan a trip to Africa once she had fully recovered. Ma responded, saying, "We should; we all should go. And even if I'm unable to make it, you should go without me. You must reconnect to our roots." She told us the family is like a tree and that we are all connected as its members, either as branches or leaves depending on our position in time. "Today, you may be a daughter, but tomorrow you will be a grandmother." Once a family member dies, she disconnects from the tree and is irreplaceable. The next family member, however, takes its source from one already connected. "That is *the tree of life*," Ma said. In a plaintive, and quivering voice, she asked, "And what is a tree without roots?" I understood what she meant. As a black American, I didn't have the ancestral knowledge of other cultures. The slave trade had disconnected my family's *Tree of Life* from its actual roots in the motherland. We had lost knowledge of our history and culture, causing us to live in the shadow of our potential.

So on September 10, 2017, when Mom called and asked, "Sonya, do you promise to find the *tree of life?*" I remembered her conviction in the hospital all those years ago. Without thinking twice, without asking *why* or *why now*, I responded, "Yes, I will. Of course, I will." And with that acquiescence, my life path would be changed forever.

Connection to the Tree of Life

According to Nicole Ellis, author of *Lost Lineage: The Quest to Identify Black Americans' Roots*, "In many cultures and among people from various nations, the act of connecting with their ancestry, kin, and heritage holds a pivotal role in shaping their identity. This intricate tapestry of heritage serves as a vessel for preserving cultural ties that extend far beyond the borders of the United States, forming lineages that instill pride and a profound sense of belonging."

"However, for Americans who can trace their roots back to enslaved Africans, the origins of their ancestry often shroud themselves in mystery. The branches of their family trees fade into obscurity after just five or six generations, serving as a stark reminder that a mere 150 years ago, black individuals were not even recognized as people in the eyes of the law."

"Genealogists have coined this conundrum as 'the brick wall,' a formidable barrier in African American lineage that can be traced back to 1870 when the federal census first began documenting African descendants. Remarkably, this was a full 250 years after they were initially transported to what would eventually become the United States. Prior to this, their existence on paper was reduced to that of another person's property. To break through this brick wall, black Americans frequently find themselves relying on the names of their ancestors' 'owners'."

For many African Americans, the deliberate severing of branches from the African American Tree of Life has resulted in a deep disconnection from our ancestors, our cultural heritage, our homeland, our native languages, our invaluable traditions – in short, from our very roots. As Mary Elliott, the curator of "Slavery and Freedom" at the National Museum of African American History and Culture, aptly remarks, "It can be a challenging endeavor for African Americans to unearth their roots and explore their heritage."

Even after the abolition of slavery, the Black experience in America has often been obscured by narratives that gloss over the darkest chapters of the nation's history. These narratives have eroded African Americans' connections to their own pasts and distorted the collective memory of the nation's historical narrative.

In Africa, the concepts of family, tribe, and reverence for elders hold immense significance. Though the connection to these values was somewhat severed for African Americans during the traumatic era of the Transatlantic Slave Trade, many families still pass down history through oral tradition. To reconnect with our lineage requires diligent research, and while modern technology has made tracing genealogy easier, conversations with the family elders is a good place to start. Some will willingly share their knowledge, while others may be more reserved. Be prepared to encounter resistance from some family members who prefer to leave certain ugly aspects of the past undisturbed. In such cases, do not be disheartened; seek out individuals who are enthusiastic about sharing their ancestral history.

I was fortunate enough to have encountered several willing sources in my own pursuit. My mother provided the name "Sarah Miller" and the birth date "1874" – which served as an excellent starting point. I knew that Sarah's parents had likely been slaves, given the historical context. I came to discover that Sarah Miller is the crux of my "Tree of Life", and I am a branch extending from her first-born son. Sarah's son Raleigh Miller is my great-grandfather, and his daughter Anglean Miller is my maternal grandmother.

Sarah had lingered in my thoughts for countless years, even before I knew anything about her, driving me to embark on an exhaustive search spanning the globe to find out more about my great-great-grand-mother. But in my journey, it soon became evident that I wasn't merely uncovering Sarah; I was also revealing the forgotten histories of my Un-Named ancestors.

The Impact of Disconnected Branches and Roots

The impact of severed branches on both enslaved individuals and free African Americans has been profound. We find ourselves in a situation where our sense of identity is fragmented, making it challenging to establish a connection with our original homeland or connect with ancestors in America and Africa. This disconnection leaves us wandering aimlessly, much like lost souls in an expansive desert, often unaware that we should actively seek a connection.

Over time, it seems as though we've been conditioned to accept this disconnected state as our inevitable fate, often failing to recognize the true value of our existence. However, it's essential to understand that rediscovering our roots can be a transformative experience. It provides us with a profound sense of belonging, re-establishes a tangible connection to our heritage, and fills the void within us, ultimately creating a profound sense of wholeness.

In my quest to uncover the story of Sarah, I embarked on a journey that would reveal aspects of myself I could have never fathomed. It was a voyage to the very soul of my ancestors, a deep dive into their endurance, their identities, and their remarkable achievements despite the oppressive circumstances they faced. I rediscovered their resilience, how they overcame every obstacle in life hurled their way, and such discovery reshaped me into someone new.

Preparing for Genealogical Research

When I first decided to reconnect with my roots, I initially focused on the Womack family, my father's lineage, in pursuit of discovering more about his ancestors. Yet, upon sharing my findings with my mother, she expressed a desire for me to delve into her family's genealogical roots. At her encouragement, I shifted my focus and embarked on the quest to trace the lineage of the woman named Sarah Miller.

My first encounter with my mother revealing insights and knowledge about our family's history marked the beginning of my journey. I never had to enlist the services of a genealogist to explore our family's past; instead, my ancestors themselves generously provided the essential clues for my research.

In my experience, most people are quite hesitant to share their family history with unfamiliar faces or outsiders. When engaging with families like the Millers and Womacks in my investigations, I often felt entrusted with classified information. Elders tended to be cautious about revealing personal details beyond their immediate family circle. Sometimes I needed introductions from my mother and aunt just to initiate a conversation with them. Interviewing the Miller elders was even more challenging, as my double Miller lineage (both maternal grandparents bearing the Miller surname) didn't automatically grant me credibility to dive into my inquiries.

One of the most daunting tasks in family history research is sifting through countless names in the National Archives and Census records databases. Identifying whether individuals with similar or identical names are indeed your own family members can be a perplexing puzzle. The solution lies in consulting a living elder who can provide crucial verification.

To research your ancestors, you must confirm vital information gathered from your elders and family stories. Armed with specific names from your family tree, you can embark on a journey of self-discovery, tracing your ancestors. Thanks to technological advancements, researching family history has become remarkably accessible. The oral and written family history my mother shared served as the pieces of the puzzle that guided my search for Sarah and the mysterious Un-Named figures in my lineage. To find your Un-Named ancestors, you'll need the wisdom of an elder—the cornerstone of your tree of life.

A Labyrinth of Sarahs

In May of 2011, I embarked on a challenging journey to uncover the hidden chapters of my family's history. My mother's mention of a mysterious figure named Sarah had ignited a spark of curiosity within me. Little did I know that this expedition would be a rollercoaster of emotions. As an African American, this quest held a profound significance beyond mere genealogy. It was an attempt to rekindle a connection to a history deliberately obscured by centuries of oppression and systemic racism.

I started by gathering family stories and anecdotes passed down through generations, akin to whispered secrets cloaked in nostalgia. These narratives, tinged with both sorrow and resilience, were the threads of a story I yearned to unravel. However, the deeper I delved, the more apparent it became that I was navigating a labyrinth with ever-shifting walls, struggling to find my way through a maze of fragmented records, erased identities, and lost connections. The sensation of being lost was overwhelming. I grappled with an intricate puzzle where pieces had been ruthlessly erased by the brutalities of slavery and the subsequent erasure of my culture and history.

Records of births, deaths, and marriages were scarce, and the names of my ancestors seemed to fade into obscurity. The knowledge that my ancestors had been treated as property rather than as individuals with stories, dreams, and aspirations haunted me. During this arduous journey, my emotions were a complex tapestry. I felt anger, a seething rage at the injustice of it all, and sadness, an enormous ache in my heart for the generations who had endured suffering, their stories buried in the sands of time. Amid the frustration and sorrow, however, there was an unyielding determination. I was resolute in my quest to unearth these hidden stories, to lend a voice to those who had been silenced for far too long. I knew the path ahead might be daunting, even seemingly impassable, but I refused to be deterred.

In this labyrinth of historical amnesia, I discovered that I was not alone. I sought solace in a community of fellow African American researchers, each of us pursuing our own threads of history, sharing discoveries, and offering support and encouragement. Together, we reclaimed our lost identities, one precious piece at a time.

By this time, Sarah Miller had captured my thoughts to the point of obsession. She stood as my ancestor, born on a plantation a mere three years after the Civil War had ended. My relentless quest for Sarah led me to Temple Square in Salt Lake City, Utah. As I boarded a flight bound for Salt Lake City, my heart brimmed with anticipation. Amidst the uncertainty that swirled within me, one thing was clear: I knew there was a library where I could delve into ancestral records. I was resolute in my determination to unveil this figure my mother had often spoken of, as well as the Caucasian Millers of Pittsylvania County – for by this time, I was vested in pursuing any information related to that family as well.

I was soon met with astonishment as I discovered a staggering 86,377 entries for "Sarah Miller" within the National Archives database. At that moment, I pondered how I could possibly narrow down this extensive list to identify the one who truly belonged to my family. It was the beginning of an intricate puzzle. Then came the moment when I found Sarah when I located her in historical records. A profound sense of ancestral continuity washed over me. It was as if a bridge had been forged through time, connecting me to a lineage that had endured unimaginable hardships. I could almost hear their whispered voices in the pages of those ancient documents, recounting tales of survival, resilience, and an unbroken spirit passed down through generations.

This newfound connection deepened my appreciation for their sacrifices and ignited a renewed determination in me to honor their legacy by continuing the pursuit of knowledge about our shared history. Standing at the crossroads of the past and the present, I felt a responsibility to carry their stories forward, ensuring that their struggles and triumphs would never be forgotten, and that they would forever be an indelible part of my identity.

I find myself repeating this statement a thousand times: if we truly understood our history, we would be profoundly transformed. History has the power to reshape who you are and how you perceive life. It grants you the ability to reach back in time and connect with something so precious that it's almost impossible to express the overwhelming pride it instills in you. As I engaged in conversations with the Miller family historians and delved into the wealth of knowledge held by the Womack historians, I was astounded by how people's eyes would light up as they recounted stories passed down through generations. These were more than just conversations; they were "brag moments." The tales their ancestors had shared wove a rich tapestry of their culture, offering them profound insights into their own identities, their roots.

I, too, was overwhelmed with a deep sense of pride and emotion as I absorbed the knowledge shared by my mother and grandfather. Yet, I was not satisfied with simply accepting what I had been told. My thirst for understanding drove me to dig deeper, to unearth more about my family's heritage, and to establish a connection with Sarah and the countless un-named ancestors who had woven their stories into the fabric of my family's history. This marked the beginning of my research journey, a path filled with curiosity and determination.

CHAPTER
TWO

The "Great Hurricane"

To grasp the significance of Sarah's story, it is crucial to recognize that her great-grandparents, or great-great-grandparents, did not choose to come to America willingly; rather, they were brutally and forcibly brought here against their wishes, forcibly separated from their homeland, which I have determined was most likely Nigeria.

The slave trade resembled a catastrophic hurricane that swept across Mother Africa, uprooting countless life trees and carrying them across the Middle Passage. This was a tempest not of weather, but of the Transatlantic Slave Trade, and it bore my ancestors as its cargo to unfamiliar lands. They were transported to the Americas, specifically to the Miller Plantation, and the Epaphrod Y. Wimbish Plantation in Pittsylvania County, Virginia, and the Nunnally and Womack plantations in Halifax County, Virginia. These plantation owners traded the precious lives of my ancestors as if they were mere commodities to cultivate tobacco in rural Virginia and they expected bountiful yields from the toil of those they enslaved.

Meanwhile, in the heartlands, coastal regions, and villages of Africa, sons and daughters wept bitterly. Their tears flowed for their beloved ones who were forcibly swept away by this devastating hurricane. The clinking of chains, the cracking of whips, and the agonizing moans and cries of men were the only sounds that filled their ears. They cried out, "For what transgressions are they subjected to this brutality, and why are they torn from their homeland?" These questions haunted their minds and yet they received no answers.

The Slave Trade

350 years. 43,600 voyages. 12.5 million Africans forced aboard European and American slave ships. 10.7 million survivors of the Middle Passage disembarked in the New World.

The most comprehensive analysis of shipping records over the course of the slave trade is the *Trans-Atlantic Slave Trade* database, edited by professors David Eltis and David Richardson. The trans-Atlantic slave trade was the largest long-distance forced movement of people in recorded history. From the sixteenth to the late nineteenth centuries, over twelve to fifteen million African men, women, and children were enslaved, transported to the Americas, and bought and sold primarily by European and Euro-American slaveholders as chattel property used for their labor and skills.

The journey to Virginia began, for countless souls, from the coast of Africa. To understand the strength required to endure such a harrowing odyssey, one must delve into the brutal reality of the transatlantic slave trade—a journey that tested the limits of human resilience, shattered the spirits of many, yet, remarkably, allowed some to emerge on the other side as survivors.

Triangular Trade from Africa to the Americas, 1650-1860.

Image from History: The Definitive Visual Guide - From the Dawn of Civilizations to the Present Day by Adam Hart-Davis

The trans-Atlantic slave trade occurred within a broader system of trade between West and Central Africa, Western Europe, and North and South America. In African ports, European traders exchanged metals, cloth, beads, guns, and ammunition for captive Africans brought to the coast from the African interior, primarily by African traders. Africans were then forcibly transported to the Americas and the West Indies to work as slaves, usually on plantations. In return, the products cultivated on these plantations – sugar, rice, tobacco, indigo, rum, and cotton – were carried back to Europe. This cycle was known as the "Triangular Trade," and the portion of it that included the acquisition and disposition of slaves is called the "Middle Passage."

The Middle Passage was a nightmarish ordeal for those who were compelled to endure it. Slave ship captains typically anchored off the Slave Coast for extended periods, ranging from a month to a year, to acquire their human cargo. Most of these individuals had been kidnapped and subjected to grueling marches to reach the coast. While it is well-known that many slaves died during the long ocean voyage, many captives also died during the long overland journeys from the interior to the coast. Out of the roughly 20 million who were taken from their homes and sold into slavery, half didn't complete the journey to the African coast, most of those dying along the way. But the worst was yet to come.

European traders held the enslaved Africans who survived the trek in fortified slave castles such as Elmina in the central region (now Ghana), Goree Island (now in present day Senegal), and Bunce Island (now in present day Sierra Leone), before forcing them into ships for the Middle Passage across the Atlantic Ocean. In the castles, the men were separated from the women, and the captors regularly raped the helpless women. The castle also featured confinement cells, small pitch-black spaces for prisoners who revolted or were seen as rebellious. Once the slaves set foot in the castle, they could spend up to three months in captivity under these dreadful conditions before being shipped off to the New World.

Throughout their time at anchor and after their departure from Africa, slaves aboard the ships faced constant threats, including attacks by hostile tribes while in port, outbreaks of disease, piracy, encounters with enemy vessels, and inclement weather. While these challenges affected both the ship's crews and the enslaved, they were even more devastating for the latter group, who also had to contend with physical, sexual, and psychological abuse at the hands of their captors.

Faced with the nightmarish conditions of the voyage and the unknown future that lay beyond, many Africans preferred to die. But even the choice of suicide was taken away from these persons. From the captain's point of view, his human cargo was extremely valuable and had to be kept alive and, if possible, uninjured. A slave who tried to starve him or herself was tortured. If torture didn't work, the slave was force fed with the help of a contraption called a speculum orum, which held the mouth open. Despite the captain's desire to keep as many slaves as possible alive, Middle Passage mortality rates were high.

But amid this darkness, a remarkable aspect of human nature emerged: resilience. The survivors found ways to support one another, forming bonds that defied the odds. It was the strength to comfort a fellow captive in their darkest hour, to share the little food and water available, to find solace in song and prayer. These acts of defiance against the dehumanizing forces of the slave trade spoke to the indomitable spirit that refused to be extinguished.

My Ancestors Survive the Middle Passage

The ancestors of Sarah Miller were seized from their home and thrust into the cruel shackles of slavery. Destined for the slave ships, Sarah's ancestors had to undergo a grueling and dangerous journey across the African interior to the Slave Coast. They had to navigate through dense forests, cross arid plains, and ford treacherous rivers—all while evading capture by rival tribes or European slavers. Every step was fraught with danger, and only the most tenacious and resourceful could hope to make it through.

As I researched my family history and reconnected with branches and roots, my journey led me to Ghana, where I visited the Cape Coast Castle, called Elmina Castle. One of the most famous castles in Ghana's dark episode of slavery, it began as a trade lodge constructed by the Portuguese in 1555 on a part of the Gold Coast, which later became known as the Cape Coast. But during my visit, I discovered a harrowing truth about its dungeons. These dark and dismal cells once held up to 1,000 male and 500 female slaves, all confined in chains and squeezed into the castle's cramped, poorly ventilated chambers. There was scarcely enough room to stretch out, and the feeble light struggled to penetrate these grim quarters. With no access to clean water or sanitation, the dungeon floors were littered with human waste, leading to the onset of severe illnesses for many captives. Astonishingly, even after 400 years, the lingering stench of human waste remained, serving as a haunting reminder of the profound cruelty that one human can inflict upon another. In the depths of my soul, I hold a steadfast belief that God allowed this odor to persist as an enduring testament to the depths of inhumanity humans are capable of.

The Elmina Slave Castle, Cape Coast, Ghana.

Photo by Sonya Womack-Miranda

During my tour of the Elmina Castle in Cape Coast Ghana, I stumbled upon a map that revealed a direct route from Elmina to Richmond, Virginia. This newfound information led me to ponder the possibility that Sarah's ancestors may have arrived in Pittsylvania County, Virginia through Richmond as a transit point. Given Richmond's significance as a prominent port, it seems plausible that these my enslaved ancestors could have been transported there, marking a crucial chapter in their journey.

Regardless of how they arrived in America, I know my ancestors were packed into ships like sardines, their humanity reduced to a mere commodity. They endured the Middle Passage and upon reaching the shores of Virginia, my family of survivors – the Womacks, the Lucks, the Millers – faced the auction block, where their worth was assessed, and their fates sealed. I spoke to a Miller descendant, an educator and historian who could recall where the building and the auction block was in Pittsylvania County, not too far from Sharswood. The inhumanity of this process was beyond comprehension, as families were torn apart, and my great grandmothers and great grandfathers were treated as chattel. My Un-Named ancestors lived on plantations where they were subjected to backbreaking labor, rape, cruel punishments, and the ever-present specter of oppression. Yet some found ways to resist, to forge communities, and to retain a semblance of their cultural heritage through language, song, and tradition.

So, what did it take for my ancestors to survive this Great Hurricane which battered their tree of life? It took unwavering determination, an unbreakable spirit, and the courage to endure. These survivors were, by necessity, the toughest of the tough. They were the ones who refused to be broken, who clung to hope in the face of despair, and who, against all odds, one day saw the light of freedom. Indeed, my grandfathers and grandmothers witnessed the dawn of freedom so that I could have the privilege of sharing their remarkable story. Their story is a testament to the enduring strength of the human spirit, a reminder that even in the darkest of times, there is a flicker of resilience that can ignite a flame of hope. The survivors of the transatlantic slave trade were not just victims; they were heroes in their own right, and their legacy continues to inspire us to this day.

CHAPTER
THREE
My Research and Discovery

Joan entrusted me with a mission: to unearth our family's rich history. Her passion for our ancestral heritage ran deep, and her stories about our past resonated in my heart. When my Miller grandfather recounted his days on the McCormick farm, I absorbed every word. The tales of the Miller plantation on Riceville Road, down the road from Riceville Baptist Church, held me in rapt attention. I hung on to every detail as my grandmother spoke of her father, affectionately known as "Pa."

Through her stories, my mother passed on invaluable information, including clues and oral family history, to help uncover the roots of our family tree. When my mother mentioned Sarah, I felt a profound sense of connection to her, despite having no idea what she looked like or any knowledge of her life. Still, I could envision Sarah through my mother's vivid descriptions. She shared stories of what she had heard about Sarah growing up in rural Virginia. I eventually had the opportunity to see the house where she lived, touching the very walls that once sheltered her. It was a profoundly moving experience.

Another source of family history was my mother's father, Charlie M. Miller or "Grandpa Dea". He was the son of Josephine Miller and Max Miller. My great-grandmother was affectionately known as "Grandma Josey." I only knew her in photographs, but my mother had the privilege of meeting her. Josephine and her husband Max served as the torchbearers of our family history, passing down their stories to their son, Charlie.

Both my mother and grandfather regaled me with tales of the Miller family's history, instilling in me a profound responsibility to preserve our heritage. My quest to uncover our ancestors began by meticulously tracing one generation back at a time, commencing with my maternal grandmother. My Miller grandfather, a dedicated historian, meticulously documented our family lineage in a seventy-year-old Bible, a cherished possession that now resides with me. His painstaking records allowed me to cross-reference and verify our ancestors on Ancestry.com.

The moment when I saw the link to the "Un-Named" marked a pivotal revelation in my journey to uncover my tree of life. My grandparents represented two consecutive generations of Millers, and my grandfather's assertion that "if you bore the surname Miller, were Black, and resided in rural Pittsylvania County, you likely had roots in the Miller plantation" proved astoundingly accurate as I painstakingly traced every Miller family member and identified a connection to Millers of Caucasian descent.

Researching the Records

While there are genealogists and services that specialize in researching family history for others, they can only do so based on the information you can provide them. So if you have the names of people in your family tree, you already possess all the necessary information to uncover your ancestors yourself, especially considering the technology available today and the records that have been made public by the National Archives. Research used to be a daunting task, involving sifting through numerous physical records or microfilm. These days Ancestry.com and other genealogical sites can do the lion's share of the work for you.

However, it is virtually impossible to find your ancestors without a thorough knowledge of your lineage and family tree. This information must come from your family or those with whom you share a connection. Having the names of individuals from your family's oral history is the first step to a successful genealogical journey. Genealogy experts suggest starting your search by examining the surname used by your ancestors in the United States Population Census. However, the accuracy of these records hinges on the information provided by your ancestors to the census takers, who went in person to each household to record the names they were told; unlike today, they were not instructed to verify the accuracy or spelling of names. Therefore, many records contain incomplete or misspelled names, so you may have to try searching multiple spellings of an ancestor's name. This underscores the significance of connecting with elder family members who can validate the names of parents, children, or spouses. However, if you lack access to elders who can corroborate names and relationships, or if they are hesitant to provide such information, your search may present more challenges.

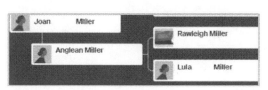

The various misspellings of my ancestors' names: "Rawleigh"

Surname	Given Name	Relationship	Gender	Race	Age
Miller	Sarah	Head	Female	Black	45
Miller	Rowley	[Son]	[Male]	[Mulatto]	25
Miller	Ella	Daughter	Female	Black	17
Miller	Meta	Daughter	Female	Black	8
Miller	Dolly	Daughter	Female	Black	6
Miller	Nimrod	Son	Male	Black	9

Throughout my search, I discovered that my great-grandfather is often spelled "Rowley" in the National Archives database.

To find Sarah, I had to start with the names and dates of people I knew were my family. I began with my maternal grandmother, Anglean Miller, but there were so many misspellings of her name, I moved on to her father. I searched the census records for "Raleigh Miller," spelled just like my uncle, but my efforts didn't yield much success. It soon became clear that the challenge lay in the fact that Raleigh's name had been recorded in census records with various spelling variations. As I mentioned, this was a common practice during that era, as census takers didn't usually ask individuals to spell their names; instead, they transcribed them based on their phonetic pronunciation. As a result, over the years Raleigh was documented as "Rollie, "Rowley," "Rawleigh," and other similar variations, making my search more complicated.

Fortunately, my mother had provided me with the names of Raleigh's children, and among them was my grandmother's sister, my great-aunt Ellen. Recognizing that "Ellen" was a more common name and less likely to be misspelled, I searched for her in the hopes that her records would eventually lead me to the correct Raleigh. However, my initial search revealed an astonishing total of 41,330 individuals named Ellen Miller. It became abundantly clear that I needed to gather additional information, clues, or family names to pinpoint the correct ancestors.

All Census & Voter Lists results for Ellen Miller

✎ ••• 1-20 of 41,330

Finally, on June 12, 2011, my breakthrough came when I finally located Ellen in the 1930 census records. Ellen's household in the census included the names of my grandmother, her siblings, and my great-grandmother Lula. This discovery led me to Raleigh Miller, the *right* Raleigh Miller, despite the misspelling of his name.

Name:	Ellan Miller	
Birth Year:		
Gender:	Female	
Race:	Negro (Black)	
Age in 1930:	4	
Birthplace:	Virginia	
Marital Status:	Single	
Relation to Head of House:	Daughter	
Home in 1930:	Banister, Pittsylvania, Virginia, USA	
Map of Home:	Banister, Pittsylvania, Virginia	
Dwelling Number:	193	
Family Number:	205	
Attended School:	No	
Father's Birthplace:	Virginia	
Mother's Birthplace:	Virginia	

Household Members	Age	Relationship
Rollie Miller	40	Head
Loula Miller	35	Wife
Eva Miller	18	Daughter
Burnett Miller	16	Son
Alma Miller	13	Daughter
Silva Miller	11	Daughter
Angeline Miller	8	Daughter

1930 Census Record. Note the copious misspellings.

1930 United States Federal Census Census	Name:	Ellan Miller	Jun 12, 2011
	Birth Year:		
	Gender:	Female	
	Race:	Negro (Black)	
	Age in 1930:	4	
	Birthplace:	Virginia	
	Marital Status:	Single	
	Relation to Head of House:	Daughter	
	Home in 1930:	Banister, Pittsylvania, Virginia, USA	
	Map of Home:	Banister,Pittsylvania,Virginia	
	Dwelling Number:	193	

It's truly indescribable the emotions that well up when you encounter your own lineage meticulously documented in the National Archives records, both profound and overwhelming in equal measure. Each time I delved into an open record that shed light on some aspect of my family's history, my thoughts immediately whisked me away to their origins.

My grandmother used to share vivid stories about Raleigh and his mother, Sarah, who resided on the mountain. Through her tales, I learned that Grandpa Raleigh was a remarkably generous man. Despite facing the challenges that came with being a

Raleigh Miller, my great-grandfather and Sarah's first-born son.

sharecropper, he managed to retain a larger portion of his harvest compared to others in similar circumstances. Raleigh's generosity extended beyond his own family; he was known for his willingness to help and support other families living on the mountain. What makes Raleigh's story even more poignant is the fact that he was just two generations removed from the era of slavery.

Sarah's grandchildren, including my grandmother, Anglean Miller, who is third from the left in the orange pants. My great-aunt Sylvia is the lady in the white skirt. I recall Aunt Sylvia Miller Womack visiting my grandmother, as she would always bring gifts. An educator by profession, she obtained a college degree. She was two generations removed from slavery. Photo by Anglean Miller

Finding Sarah of Sharswood

Though I had a solid lead on Raleigh's whereabouts, I didn't immediately dive into the search for Sarah. Life happened, and my research was pushed to the wayside.

I accepted a new position in Washington, D.C., working for the Superior Courts of the District of Columbia, an action which caused a significant shift in my life. My responsibilities in this new training role demanded substantial time, both during and after regular work hours. Additionally, my daughter, who was then a vibrant and active 7-year-old, occupied much of my attention. Consequently, the demands of my professional life and the responsibilities of parenthood left me with limited opportunities to delve into genealogical research during that period. It took several years before I found myself circling back to my genealogical research and resuming the quest to trace Sarah's history. This is one of the intriguing aspects of research; it often unfolds in sync with the events and priorities of our lives. Finally, in 2014, I found a moment to catch my breath, and I eagerly resumed the search for Sarah.

The vastness of a national database can make it feel like searching for a needle in a haystack. The most crucial avenue for uncovering ancestors lies in connecting with a living oral historian who possesses intimate knowledge of the family and its descendants. This step is essential for confirming the individuals you've added to your family tree. Unfortunately, this is where the search ends for some of us – if you don't have living family members with long memories, you may be unable to verify which name among thousands belongs to your tree of life.

Standing near Raleigh's home in Virginia.

Photo by Sonya Womack-Miranda

I was lucky. At the time of my research, I had spoken to many family members on both my father's and mother's sides, and in both cases, I was able to validate names and dates of family ancestors through these conversations with elders from both branches of the family.

I knew a search for "Sarah Miller" – two very common names – would return hundreds of thousands of results. To narrow down my records search, I focused on Bannister County, Virginia. Sarah's age I derived from her tombstone, which I had discovered at our family's Riceville Baptist Church in Java, Virginia. Birth dates can be found on tombstones if you happen to know where family members are buried, although I later learned they weren't always completely accurate. During census data collection, birth dates might vary by one to seven years. Therefore, I included the birth date range of 1868 to 1874. Despite these parameters, there were still 86,377 results for "Sarah Miller" in "Bannister County, Virginia" in "1874." By refining my search to Black females, the count reduced to 6,999 Sarah Millers. Still, I knew I needed to include additional names or dates to actually find my Sarah.

It was my mother who played the pivotal role in my eventual success by supplying the defining clues. She told me of Sarah's sons – Raleigh, Nimrod (called Nimmie), and Gideon, who was tragically killed early in life in a farming accident on the McCormick farm in rural Java, Virginia. The 1910 census eventually yielded a positive identification, with Sarah listed as head of the household, along with two sons "Rowley" and "Nimrod."

Surname	Given Name	Relationship	Gender	Race	Age
Miller	Sarah	Head	Female	Black	45
Miller	Rowley	[Son]	[Male]	[Mulatto]	25
Miller	Ella	Daughter	Female	Black	17
Miller	Meta	Daughter	Female	Black	8
Miller	Dolly	Daughter	Female	Black	6
Miller	Nimrod	Son	Male	Black	9

Armed with these names and Sarah's approximate birth date pulled from the 1910 census, I combed through the Social Security Applications and Claims Index to see if I could find additional proof this was my Sarah Miller. And there they were.

I now possessed conclusive evidence, supported by two documents, suggesting that Sarah was likely born around 1868, three years after the Civil War.

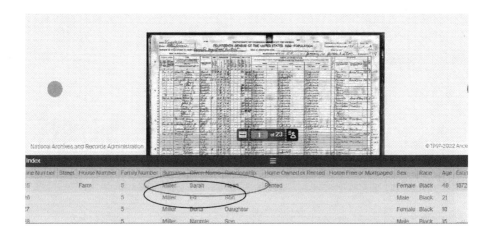

Flush with success, I searched successive census records, tracking Sarah's life through the years. I found her in the 1920 census, and again in the 1940 census. Though her birthdate continued to fluctuate in the records, the names of her children remained a constant, proving this was my Sarah. I also discovered a marriage record for Sarah Miller to Davis Miller.

Virginia, Select Marriages, 1785-1940
Birth, Marriage, & Death

Name:	Sarah Miller
Gender:	Female
Spouse:	Davis Miller
Child:	Nimmie Miller

Aug 30, 2018

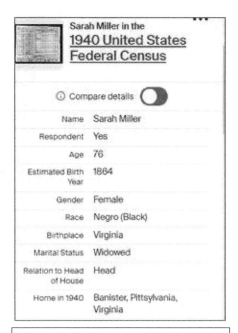

Sarah Miller in the

1940 United States Federal Census

ⓘ Compare details ◯

Name	Sarah Miller
Respondent	Yes
Age	76
Estimated Birth Year	1864
Gender	Female
Race	Negro (Black)
Birthplace	Virginia
Marital Status	Widowed
Relation to Head of House	Head
Home in 1940	Banister, Pittsylvania, Virginia

And I discovered that by the age of 76, my great-great-grandmother was widowed.

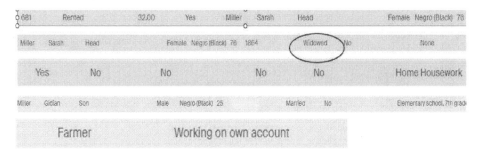

This treasure trove of documentation solidified by certainty that this woman, *this* Sarah Miller, was the core of my tree of life. I proudly added her to my records and my family history, full of conflicting emotions but an overarching sense of accomplishment.

The Emotion of Finding Sarah

The Church of Jesus Christ of Latter-day Saints' Family History Library in Salt Lake City, Utah, is the world's most extensive genea-

logical library open to the public. By the time I renewed my genealogy research in 2014, I knew I needed to visit this amazing resource
in Temple Square. June 12, 2014 found me perusing historical documents at the Family History Library where I stumbled upon a
wealth of information about my ancestors that left me in awe. As I
scrolled through digital
pages with trembling
hands, I felt as though I
was on a sacred quest.

Initially, my search
had seemed fruitless,
but the voice of Sarah
Miller from Sharswood
remained persistent in
my mind, encouraging
me to persevere and
explore our family his-
tory through various
methods. I believed it was the spirit of Sarah Miller guiding me to
find her in the historic pages. I viewed this entire endeavor to trace
my tree of life as a spiritual one, as if I were seeking the living among
the departed, for surely Sarah's soul could not find peace knowing
her children might be disconnected from their heritage. It was as if
her voice echoed in my spirit, urging me to share her story and reveal
the family tree she had helped cultivate.

It was around 1:30 p.m. on that day that I finally discovered
Sarah Miller of the Sharswood Plantation, the woman I had been
diligently seeking for years. Every crucial detail about her unfolded
before my eyes. I wept uncontrollably, repeating, "Oh my goodness!
I have found
Sarah." She stood
before me through
genealogical rec-
ords, and I couldn't
contain my tears
of joy and sor-

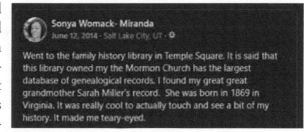

Relationship to me

Sarah Miller 1868-1949
2nd great-grandmother
⌄
Raleigh Miller
Son of Sarah Miller
⌄
Angliane Miller
Daughter of Raleigh H. Miller
⌄
Joan B. Miller Womack
Daughter of Angliane Miller
⌄
sonya womack
You are the daughter of Joan B. Miller Womack

Sonya Womack- Miranda
June 12, 2014 · Salt Lake City, UT · ✿

Went to the family history library in Temple Square. It is said that
this library owned my the Mormon Church has the largest
database of genealogical records. I found my great great
grandmother Sarah Miller's record. She was born in 1869 in
Virginia. It was really cool to actually touch and see a bit of my
history. It made me teary-eyed.

row. Through her records I witnessed the remarkable life of a woman who had paved the way for my freedom and liberty in America, the vital part of my lineage. It was an overwhelming experience, akin to a profound vision, with an angelic message of hope and joy. I felt both misery for the suffering my ancestors endured, and joy for finding my roots and connecting with ancestors who defined my identity.

Sarah's Story: The Millers and the Womacks

"Parallel Lives, Divergent Fates: Sarah Miller and William G. Womack in Post-Civil War America"

Sarah D. Miller, my second great-grandmother, was born in 1868, just three years after the Civil War. My paternal great grandfather William G. Womack shared her same birth year of 1868. William's father, an unnamed slave in the census records and in slave schedules, was born in 1842. Sarah's father, an unnamed slave, was recorded as born around 1820. Williams's grandfather, another unnamed slave, was born around 1800.

William Womack and Sarah Miller both stood as one generation removed from slavery. Their parents had endured slavery, their ancestors had survived the harrowing journey across the Atlantic. These shared experiences form the unique bond between them. However, it is the post-slavery experiences of William's family that stand out, substantiated by both oral family narratives and meticulously researched and official recorded court deed records.

By 1910, William not only owned his home outright but is also listed as a farmer, not a sharecropper in census records, signifying that he had individuals working for him. Oral family history and court deed records provide solid evidence that my great-grandfather managed to acquire a substantial 200-acre parcel of rural land in Halifax County, Virginia in 1895. William was also able to read and write and attended school. This remarkable achievement becomes even more impressive when you consider his background as the son of a former slave. Born in 1868, he would have been twenty in 1888. Within a mere seven short years, he demonstrated remarkable determination and resourcefulness to secure this extensive piece of land. (I was taken to this land by my first cousin Richard Valon Womack where I stood up on his truck and looked out over the land, and I find it impossible to convey in this book just how profoundly impactful and awe-inspiring it is.)

A particularly noteworthy aspect that distinguishes my great-grandfather William from others in my family tree is the existence of a unique historical document providing proof of how William acquired the 200 acres of land. The answer lies within the will of a slave owner in Halifax County with whom the Womack family shared a uniquely intimate relationship.

William and his father are both identified as "mulatto" in census records, a now-dated term used to describe people who were ethnically Caucasian and African American. All official records consistently classify my fourth great-grandfather, his mother, and their descendants as mulatto. This distinctive link may offer valuable insights into the reasons the Womack descendants were able to attain landownership. This assertion is corroborated by both family lore and court documents, which suggest that this group of African Americans, this branch of the Womack family, achieved a notable level of prosperity. My great-grandfather William accumulated wealth, it becomes evident from court records I have obtained that my Womack ancestors enjoyed distinct opportunities not afforded to Sarah and her family by their slaveowners.

Unlike the affluent Womacks, Sarah lived her life as a farm laborer. Sarah could not read or write. By the year 1910, at the age of forty-five, she had become a mother to sons by Davis Miller. She became widowed somewhere between 1920 and 1930. By this point, she was a mother to seven children. Following her husband's passing, Sarah Miller took on the roles of both breadwinner and the head of the family by continuing to work the land, as her parents had before her.

In a document currently held at the University of North Carolina's Davis Library, authored by Nathaniel Crenshaw Miller, the owner of the Sharswood plantation, it is recorded that on August 9, 1868, Sarah's parents entered into a contract to remain on the

Sharswood plantation with their family, long after the official end of slavery. Sarah herself was just five months old at that time, having been born on the Sharswood plantation. Sarah's parents elected to continue working on the very plantation where they had previously been enslaved.

I have often found myself deep in thought, contemplating the choices made by my unnamed Miller great-grandparents on that momentous day. I have wondered about the true price or cost of their new found freedom. Yes, they had been liberated from the physical shackles of slavery, but what awaited them on the other side? What were they truly prepared to do after the end of slavery? In essence they were free, but what did that freedom entail? Without an education or support networks they were free to starve, free to eke out a meager existence, free to scrape together whatever scraps they could from their former slave masters – and what kind of life was that?

These narratives of the contrasting lives of the Millers and Womacks serve as poignant reminders of the intricate nature of the African American journey in the wake of emancipation. They vividly illustrate how determination and ambition frequently clashed with entrenched systemic obstacles and economic limitations. Sarah and William stand as embodiments of the multifarious facets of this historical epoch. William, it seems, carved out a trajectory of advancement in the face of bewildering discrimination and constricted opportunities, while Sarah's family continued to endure a life of hardship and labor on the very plantation that once held them in bondage.

Decades later, my grandfather Charlie would recount his own experiences toiling on the McCormick farm and the McGregor farm in Pittsylvania County, Virginia. He vividly described how at the close of each harvest season, there was absolutely nothing to show for their backbreaking labor. He lamented that most farmers, despite their relentless efforts, ended up owing money and rarely man-aged to accumulate anything substantial. This was the life that my Un-Named great-grandparents had chosen on that fateful day in 1868.

The questions persist: Was this the true essence of freedom for them? Had they merely exchanged one form of servitude for another?

The struggles they encountered in the post-slavery era painted a complex picture of the challenges and uncertainties that accompanied their newfound liberty. Yet, they endured, and their choices, though undoubtedly difficult, stood as a testament to their unwavering resilience and their unwavering commitment to carving out a brighter future for themselves and the generations that would follow.

While Sarah Miller, due to her youth, may not have personally witnessed the most extreme atrocities faced by enslaved Black people working on plantations, she undoubtedly felt the enduring impacts of slavery even after its official abolition. She would have observed the nation's journey toward reconstruction following the Civil War, a tumultuous period marked by conflict between its Northern and Southern regions. Her mother, who had endured a lifetime of enslavement since childhood, would likely have recounted some of their enslavement experiences to her. This was the history passed down through my grandparents, cousins, and my mother Joan.

Sarah and her entire family were devout Christians, actively participating in the congregations of Riceville Missionary Baptist Church and Mt. Airy Baptist Church in Java and Mt. Airy, Virginia. It is likely that her parents introduced her to God and the church, instilling in her a sense of gratitude for the freedom and liberty granted to their generation. Each day, the Black community would gather in prayer, seeking solace and offering prayers for the souls of those who had perished in rebellion against their slave masters, as well as for all the Black lives lost during the era of slavery.

In her later years, Sarah might have been fervently praying for the survival and prosperity of her children and generations yet unborn—a testament to the enduring love of a mother who wishes to see her children achieve more than she ever could, despite the challenges they faced. It appears that Sarah's line of Millers did not fare as well as my great-grandfather William Womack did in the post-slavery era. The contrasting experiences of these two families reflect the diverse paths that African American families took following the abolition of slavery. While my great-grandfather William was able to achieve some degree of success as a farmer and landowner, Sarah Miller faced her own unique challenges and circumstances. These differences highlight the complex and varied narratives within the African American community during that period.

Half of Sarah's life had been spent in or near the slave cabins on the Sharswood Plantation, not as a slave but as a farm laborer earning wages. The enduring slave cabin still stands today, bearing witness to her legacy for her great-grandchildren and serving as a tangible testament to the remarkable woman that Sarah Miller was in the history of the Black race in America.

Touching the Walls of Sarah's Soul

Visiting my great-great-grandmother's house for the first time was an extremely emotional and eye-opening experience. I had heard stories about her, but actually standing in the place where she had lived and breathed brought history to life in a way I could never have imagined. As I approached the weathered, modest house nestled on a piece of land in the woods, a mix of anticipation and trepidation filled my heart. The small wooden structure stood as a testament to resilience, bearing the weight of countless stories and memories.

Sarah's presence lingered in every corner of that house. I could almost hear her voice, soft and wise, telling stories of her life, the struggles she endured, and the resilience she embodied. I imagined her preparing meals over the open flame of the wood heaters, her hands worn but capable, her spirit unbreakable.

Touching the walls, I couldn't help but feel an intense connection to her and the countless others who had lived through the horrors of post slavery and life on a plantation during and after slavery. The rough wooden boards, once coated in layers of paint, now bore the marks of time and history. I traced my fingers along the faded surfaces, wondering if she had done the same, seeking solace in the tangible reminder of her existence.

As I explored the surrounding property, I was overcome with a mixture of emotions. A sense of pride swelled within me, knowing that my great grandmother had found strength within these very walls. Her resilience and determination to endure unimaginable hardships were palpable in every inch of the land. Yet, there was also a deep sadness that washed over me—a sorrow for the injustices she and so many others had endured, and a reminder of the enduring legacy of slavery in my family's history.

Standing in my great grandmother's house, I felt a deep connection to my roots, a complex mix of pride and pain. It was a sobering reminder of the strength of the human spirit and the enduring legacy of those who had come before me. The house may have been a relic of the past, but it echoes of history would forever shape my understanding of who I was and where I came from.

Photos by Sonya
Womack-Miranda

As I peered through the windows of Sarah's house that day, I sensed the presence of her soul, whispering that I had arrived and forged a connection with her. It felt as though she had foreseen that one of her descendants would come seeking her, hoping to reestablish a link to the roots of Sarah Miller. I spoke to Sarah and shared these words:

"As I embraced these timeworn and resilient walls, I can sense your presence, Sarah. I feel your anguish, your aspirations, and your silent burdens. Most importantly, I feel the resurgence of your unwavering strength. These walls, battered and barren, serve as a poignant mirror reflecting the years I've yearned for a connection with you. Your dwelling, still standing proudly, serves as a testament to your indomitable spirit—an enduring legacy you've bequeathed for me to uncover. You had an earnest desire for us, your descendants, to witness a window into your life with our own eyes. You left behind a milestone, a tangible structure for me to touch, affirming your very existence. I'm committed to sharing your narrative, Sarah. I have forged through a long and arduous journey to find you. But it won't be just your story alone; I aim to recount the tale of how I unearthed you, alongside the stories of the Un-Named Miller slaves of Pittsylvania County, Virginia."

Sarah the Survivor

Despite the odds stacked against her, Sarah laid an unbreakable foundation for my freedom and prosperity. This legacy can never be shattered or taken away; it will forever be honored by her descendants. Every generation stemming from her lineage will be intimately acquainted with her remarkable deeds and the sacrifices she made to provide us with the cherished lives we now lead.

The slave masters aimed to dehumanize my ancestors, believing they could strip away the very essence of life. Stories have been passed down of the cruelties of slavery, and post slavery. Oral family history as told by my great aunt Jennie Womack Tucker states that a slave owner's wife had one of my Un-Named ancestors' teeth knocked out to disfigure him. The oral narrative passed down through generations stated that the mulatto child had been so beautiful and loved to smile. It's possible that the child was her husband's son, and this situation may have filled her with such anger and resentment that she felt compelled to inflict a lifelong disfigurement upon him. Frequently, in the historical context, when slave owners fathered children with enslaved individuals, those offspring were typically subject to sale. In this particular case, however, the slave owner exhibited a different approach. He chose to retain all of his mixed-race slaves and even formally acknowledged two of them as his own children in official census records.

We must share Sarah's story and all of these stories of our Un-Named with the next generation to inspire and ignite the strength and courage within them. Our history, even the painful and difficult parts, must not be hidden and it's not a cause for embarrassment. It is our story, and it is essential that it is told and passed down for gener-ations to come. By understanding where we come from and the long line of fearless people who came before us, we can share and inspire the next generation. This will help them to better compre-hend who they are and draw strength from their ancestors' resilience and deter-mination.

These stories are a testament to the enduring spirit of our peo-ple and the unwavering pursuit of freedom and justice. The slave master did not understand or recognize that the **African spirit is a force mightier than anything on this earth, and it can only be sub-dued by the divine force that created us, God Himself.**

CHAPTER
FOUR

Unraveling the Clues: The Sarah-Sharswood Connection

"Researching information about slaves involves delving into various historical documents such as tax records, estate records, slave schedules, and wills," explains Mary Elliott, curator of "Slavery and Freedom" at the National Museum of African American History and Culture. She emphasizes that even after the abolition of slavery, the Black community has faced efforts to conceal the darkest chapters of American history, weakening the connection of African Americans to their ancestral past and distorting the nation's collective memory. This disconnection from their roots began during the era of slavery and persists today, with numerous stories of African Americans losing their loved ones and their ancestral ties.

From 1790 to 1860, slaves were counted in federal census records. However, as they were seen merely as property, they were not named, recorded only by age, color, gender as "Female, Mulatto, 16" or "Male, Black, 45." It was the 1870 census where everyone was finally named, even if, as I discovered in my own research, the names weren't always correctly recorded. Researchers today who go looking for their unnamed ancestors must refer to the 1860 and 1850 slave schedules, which provide information about each slave's gender, age, and color, listed under the owner's name. But this method presents an additional problem – it requires knowing the identity of the slave owner. So throughout my journey to discover my ancestors, I affectionately refer to these no-named individuals as the Un-Named.

My intent is to breathe life into their names, ensuring that they are no longer consigned to obscurity and insignificance.

The Power of a Name

As I embarked on the journey of writing this book, my initial enthusiasm stemmed from a profound desire to share my personal experiences in discovering Sarah Miller and my tree of life. However, as I delved into historical records, I soon found myself navigating an emotional rollercoaster. Within those records, I unearthed deliberate omissions of names that were undeniably painful to see. These discoveries ignited profound questions that continued to occupy my thoughts. Why were these names purposefully omitted? What significance lay behind this deliberate act? As an African American, I couldn't help but ponder why establishing a connection with my ancestors and discovering their names was such a challenge. Why had their identities been left unrecorded? In one particularly remarkable instance, I traced the ancestry of my seventh-generation grandfather, who happened to be of Caucasian descent, all the way to 17th-century England. This stark contrast in the preservation of records between enslaved individuals and their Caucasian counterparts left me both perplexed and deeply contemplative.

Thomas ANDERSON Sr
BIRTH 10 FEB 1732 • Northumberland, England
DEATH 20 SEP 1794 • Pleasant Level, Hanover, Virginia
7th great-grandfather

Why the Omissions of Names?

The concealment of the past, lineage, and connection to the ancestral homeland of enslaved African Americans in the United

States can be understood as a deliberate strategy employed by slave masters and the American slave system for several reasons:

Dehumanization: Slavery was built on the dehumanization of enslaved people. By erasing their history, culture, and connections to their homeland, slave owners could more effectively perpetuate the idea that enslaved individuals were property rather than human beings with rights and heritage. Stripping them of their identity and history made it easier to justify the inhumane treatment they endured.

Control: By severing enslaved individuals from their roots and ancestral ties, slave masters could exert greater control over them. Enslaved people who were disconnected from their cultural and familial heritage were less likely to organize, resist, or rebel, as they lacked a collective sense of identity and belonging.

Psychological Manipulation: The erasure of ancestral connections was a form of psychological manipulation. Enslaved people were often forced to adopt the culture, language, and religion of their captors, further distancing them from their African heritage. This helped perpetuate the idea that they were inferior and should be subservient.

Fear of Uprisings: Slave owners were often fearful of insurrections and revolts, which had occurred in various forms throughout American history. By keeping enslaved individuals ignorant of their history and heritage, slave masters believed they could reduce the risk of coordinated resistance efforts.

Economic Interests: Slavery was an economic institution, and slave owners sought to maximize their profits. Keeping enslaved individuals ignorant of their heritage and lineage made it easier to buy and sell them as commodities without considering their familial or cultural ties.

Preservation of Social Order: The broader society at the time was built on a foundation of white supremacy. Revealing the connections between enslaved people and their African heritage could challenge this social order and lead to questions about the morality of slavery.

It's important to note that while slave masters and the American slave system attempted to erase these connections, enslaved individuals often found ways to preserve their cultural and familial ties through oral traditions, music, religious practices, and other forms of resistance. Over time, these efforts contributed to the preservation and eventual celebration of African American culture and heritage. Today, many people and organizations actively work to uncover and celebrate the ancestral connections and history of African Americans who were enslaved in the United States.

For some, the past holds such unthinkable pain that it can seem tempting to bury one's head in the sand and pretend it doesn't exist. Others carry the weight of shame associated with a lineage forged in the crucible of slavery, knowing that they are descendants of ancestors who may have suffered unimaginable cruelty, including the possibility of rape by their slave masters—a truth too painful to fully comprehend. I say to those who are ashamed, the ancestors wanted more, our great-grandmother aspired to build families, raise children with husbands in loving homes. However, the harsh reality was that they had no control over their lives during slavery, and even after its abolition.

It's crucial for us to honor their journey, gain a deep understanding of it, and pass this knowledge down to the next generation. Yes, it is crucial that we never forget our past, remember our origins, and understand that it is our collective journey.

Our ancestors endured the harrowing trials of the Great Hurricane, the Middle Passage, Transatlantic Slave voyage, which makes us descendants of some of the strongest people alive. Sarah D. Miller and William G. Womack exemplified this unyielding spirit, and I am proud to possess that same spirit because I know who they are.

I frequently ponder the remarkable resilience of those who endured the horrors of slavery while managing to keep their minds intact. There was a powerful force within them, burning so intensely, that it enabled generation after generation to hold on tenaciously, striving to reach what they perceived as the promised land of freedom. I believe that their ability to do so stemmed from their unwavering connection to something from their past, be it their culture, traditions, or beliefs from their native land – or their family names.

There are no official records of the Un-Named enslaved man who is part of my family tree, born in 1842. My cousin also has Un-Named grandparents who, despite my painstaking search through countless hours and years of records, remain Un-Named still. Like many slave-owners at the time, the Miller slaveowners did not record the names of their enslaved individuals – a practice which made my research all the more difficult. Had they recorded the names of their slaves, I would possess a clearer understanding of my Miller ancestors and the identities of those who rest in the Sharswood slave burial ground.

Fortunately for me, my family engaged in the practice of oral storytelling, and I was able to glean clues and starting points from the tales I heard throughout my childhood. My father is the one who, eventually, revealed to me the name "Green Womack" and led me to the enslaved in our family.

Charlie "Dea" Miller, the Storyteller

My memories of my Miller grandfather take me back to my childhood in rural Pittsylvania County, where I fondly remember riding on the back of his truck on trips to Chatham, Virginia. It was a time etched in my heart forever. Despite not having much in terms of material wealth, Grandpa Dea displayed his generosity by taking all his grandchildren to the store, handing each of us a nickel to buy candy at Stone McGregor's store, on 832.

My grandfather transitioned from sharecropping to employment at Dan River Mills in Danville, Virginia, where he eventually achieved the dream of owning his own home. Throughout my upbringing, my grandfather instilled in me the belief that I could attend college, a notion I sometimes considered far-fetched. When the time came for me to pursue higher education, I had my heart set on either Florida A&M or Norfolk State University, where his daughter Althea had also attended. Unfortunately, I didn't receive enough financial aid for either institution. Undeterred, Grandpa Dea took me to the only black-owned bank, First State Bank in Danville, Virginia, where he introduced me to the manager. It was through this connection that I was able to secure a loan, enabling me to attend Norfolk State University.

Had my grandfather not shared his history and journey in this country with me, I might have remained adrift on my own path. Grandpa Dea bore no shame about his past as a sharecropper; he saw it as an essential chapter in his life's story. His existence was fueled by the aspiration to witness the succeeding generation flourish, yearning for a brighter tomorrow. In his eyes, I embodied that future.

If we fail to pass down our history, share our journey, and uncover the names of our ancestors, we inadvertently embrace the notion that our own worthiness is not deserving of knowledge about our heritage. We resign ourselves to a disconnection from our true identities. In doing so, we leave our children with nothing to grasp as a source of inspiration for progress and advancement in the generations to come. Perhaps these were the thoughts running through my granddad's mind as he shared his passion for culture, family, history, and his own life's journey.

Charlie Miller's enduring legacy serves as a source of inspiration for me, motivating me to encourage fellow African Americans to diligently record their own histories and ensure their transmission to the next generation. Beyond Charlie, other Miller elders have also been wellsprings of inspiration on my journey. Though these Miller ancestors and historians have left this earthly realm, they entrusted me with the solemn responsibility of preserving our invaluable history.

A younger Charlie Max Miller pictured at the lectern of Riceville Missionary Baptist Church. My grandfather hailed from a family of sharecroppers; he, too, later engaged in sharecropping. In addition to his farming work, he was a Freemason.

As a child, I unknowingly absorbed the stories that unfolded around me, like a silent recorder capturing the rich tapestry of my family's history. Grandpa Dea, a masterful storyteller, spun tales of his own upbringing on the farm, often interweaving the threads of our ancestral heritage into his narratives. He possessed a remarkable ability to breathe life into the past, effortlessly recounting stories of generations long gone. His tales were not merely anecdotes; they were gateways to our family's past, revealing the lives and struggles of our ancestors. Among the myriad of anecdotes, he sprinkled clues about the Miller plantation, igniting a spark of curiosity within me.

It was my grandfather's storytelling that initially planted the seeds of genealogical curiosity in my heart. His captivating stories served as a beckoning call to explore our family's roots. This curiosity would later take hold of my mother Joan, who was equally passionate about our Miller heritage, Black history, and the broader tapestry of African history. Her fervor for uncovering our roots was infectious and invigorating.

It's difficult for me to convey the depth of my obsession with tracing our ancestry, a passion ignited by my mother's unwavering encouragement. Grandpa Dea, in his own quiet way, had provided the initial clues. Among his treasured possessions, he left behind a time-worn, 70-year-old Bible, a sacred relic in which he meticulously inscribed the names of our ancestors. Among the names etched into its pages, one stood out—Rosie Miller, his grandmother, a slave. This was another precious fragment of our history and encouraged me to discover the stories of Rosie and her husband, Charles, also a slave. Their names served as the key that unlocked the door to a world of history concealed within my grandfather's tales, a world that awaited my exploration with bated breath.

Image of Charlie Max Miller and his daughter Joan Miller Womack. My grandfather frequently called Sharswood the Miller Plantation, highlighting the significance of our family's history. This understanding has been openly passed down through generations within our family. In our family bible, the names of my second great-grandparents, Rosie and Charles, were preserved. They were both enslaved on the Sharswood Plantation. Surprisingly, I didn't need to search for them on ancestry; the platform automatically linked them to me through my grandfather and his parents.

Charles Miller

BIRTH Virginia

DEATH

sources (1)

Family Info

Father	Charles Miller (1824–)
Mother	
Spouse	Rosie Miller (1830–)
Children	Max (1894–1930)

The Gatekeepers

It's essential to grasp the presence of certain individuals within your family whom I would refer to as the "gatekeepers." They hold the keys to your family's history, possessing intimate knowledge of our ancestral past. However, they guard this knowledge closely and are hesitant to divulge it. Perhaps this generation bears a sense of shame or believes that a veil of secrecy should shroud certain aspects of our history, compelling them to withhold these precious stories for reasons that elude me. My Father's family, the Womacks and Lucks, were very open with my history. My maternal grandfather shared his history, but some family members can be closed and secretive. Might there be a rationale for the veil of secrecy?

Engaging in discussions about ancestry and genealogy is a fascinating journey for me, and it's remarkable how it can reveal hidden stories within every family. It's true that secrets, whether big or small, seem to be a common thread in most family histories. These secrets can encompass various aspects of family life, from hidden relationships and undisclosed origins to untold hardships and long-lost connections. Exploring one's genealogy often unveils these hidden narratives and adds depth and complexity to the family's overall history. It's a reminder that every family has its own unique and sometimes mysterious tapestry of stories waiting to be uncovered and understood.

I distinctly remember an encounter with a gentleman who shared a remarkable tale with me. Despite his outward Caucasian appearance, he revealed his identity as an African American. His narrative painted a vivid picture of his family's history, one that unfolded on the Eastern Shore of Maryland. He had embarked on a quest to trace his roots and, in the process, unearthed a startling revelation. He uncovered that his ancestors had resided in a town where they had attended the sole African American school in the aftermath of slavery. What made this revelation even more astonishing was the fact that they had, for all intents and purposes, "passed" as Caucasian, a practice many engaged in at the turn of the twentieth century to conceal their true African American heritage and enjoy the benefits of living in the community as white.

The gentleman recounted a pivotal moment when the secret came dangerously close to exposure. It was discovered that records detailing their attendance at the black school were stored at a local courthouse. However, before the truth could be unveiled, an inexplicable tragedy occurred: the courthouse was mysteriously reduced to ashes, with every single document and record obliterated beyond recovery. This ominous turn of events sheds light on one of the underlying reasons why many people are so reticent and guarded when it comes to sharing their African American family histories.

In my own journey of exploring my ancestry, I found myself inundated with inquiries from genealogists, particularly after my appearance on 60 Minutes, wanting to assist me with tracing my family's lineage. I pondered how these dedicated professionals could possibly unravel the intricate threads of my family's history if they were unable to converse with my family members and glean first-hand insights into our ancestors. It became abundantly clear that even for a member of the family, obtaining such information was a nearly insurmountable challenge. The gatekeepers of one's family often conspire to keep these ancestral narratives hidden in the shadows, elusive and enigmatic.

The gatekeepers have good intentions – they wish to keep the family from scandal and ruin and loss. However, they remain unaware that their actions inadvertently contribute to our sense of being lost and disconnected, leaving us wandering in the wilderness of our ancestry. They may not realize the significance of what they withhold—an essential key to defining our self-worth, fostering self-love, and establishing a profound connection to our heritage.

Alberta Miller Womack, the Historian

Despite the best efforts of the well-meaning but misguided gatekeepers, my perseverance in finding family members willing to discuss Sarah's Miller's history paid off when I encountered Alberta Elizabeth Miller Womack. Meeting my eighty-five-year-old cousin for the first time was an unforgettable experience. She held the esteemed title of being the Miller family's exclusive historian and was genuinely thrilled to learn about my keen interest in our family's history.

Alberta stood as a beacon of openness amidst a landscape of guarded secrets. She was the antithesis of the gatekeepers, who often cloaked our family's history in secrecy. When I first connected with Alberta, her enthusiasm to unveil the Miller family's history was palpable. Unlike those who withheld their knowledge, Alberta possessed a genuine eagerness to share the abundant tapestry of stories and experiences that comprised our family's legacy.

We crossed paths in the summer of 2017, and during that momentous meeting, she unveiled family history that would forever bind us together. Alberta had a peculiar way of sharing stories, often offering just half of the narrative. Occasionally, she'd say, "I've given you enough for today," leaving me curious and prompting me to request the continuation of the tale. She'd playfully respond, "No, come back, and I'll share the rest of it. What I'm about to tell you might be too much to digest all at once." I'd chuckle and promise to return another time. It's a curious paradox that families hold rich tales, yet much of this history remains concealed, untold. I was consistently captivated by the stories Alberta recounted. Afterward, I'd turn to my Aunt Althea Miller, cross-referencing some of Alberta's narratives, and consistently, she'd corroborate their authenticity. These stories had been passed down from Alberta's father, who was my grandmother's uncle.

Alberta possessed a wealth of Miller family history knowledge and an extensive collection of family photographs spanning decades. She was the only relative who had the sole picture of my second great-grandmother, Sarah Miller. She had so many pictures. Our meetings over two summers in Chatham, Virginia, provided me with a lifetime of cherished memories. As Alberta learned about my research, she invited me to her home, where we sat down on cool summer days and discussed our family history. I avidly documented her stories while listening to her speak about our ancestors. My excitement made it challenging to jot down notes. However, she made a request that I couldn't resist. She asked me to locate Sarah's parents, about whom she knew nothing, not even their names.

The Un-Named, Slaves to the Sharswood Planation

Starting in 1790, the United States Federal Census was conducted every decade, with the primary objective of counting every individual (except for Native Americans). As noted earlier, from 1790 to 1860, enslaved individuals were only recorded under the names of their enslavers, not afforded the dignity of being identified by their given names. Knowing this, I realized that the 1870 census records might hold valuable information to help me fulfill Cousin Alberta's request, even though Sarah herself would have been a very young child at that time. Sadly, these records did not bear any trace of Nimmie and Raleigh, the crucial clues my mother had provided to help locate Sarah's lineage. Faced with the daunting task of sifting through vast archives with limited information to go on, I scoured National Archives records. The quest to find these unnamed individuals proved to be an exceedingly challenging endeavor.

It was during this period that I turned to Alberta for guidance and shared my mounting concerns, expressing the near impossibility of locating Sarah's parents without even their initials. All we knew was that the Un-Named Miller slaves, Sarah's parents, were born into slavery around 1820. In her wisdom, Alberta emphasized the importance of interviewing elderly relatives within our family before their precious knowledge vanished, highlighting the paramount significance of preserving our shared history. I reached out to my maternal grandmother's sister who was close to 100 years old, but she would not discuss family history.

Without insight into Sarah and her siblings, I would have been lost amidst a sea of data, confronted with an overwhelming 186,000 Sarah Millers in Pittsylvania County, Virginia. I had found an older Sarah Miller in the census data, accompanied by her sons R. Miller and Nimmie, but it became evident that I needed to locate an infant Sarah Miller who had yet to bear children. The elusive nature of her siblings further complicated matters, with no information available from my mother to provide a breakthrough.

Alberta shared two invaluable clues that proved to be the breakthrough I needed. She mentioned Sarah's siblings, Harrison and Charity, and with those connections I stumbled upon a 1-year-old Sarah Miller in the 1870 census.

Name	Sarah Miller
Age in 1870	[1]
Birthplace	Virginia
Dwelling Number	737
Home in 1870	Subdivision North of Dan River, Pittsylvania, Virginia
Race	Black
Gender	Female
Post Office	Riceville and Peytonsburg
Occupation	At Home

Household Members (Name)	Age
David Miller	60
Violet Miller	40
Henry Miller	15
Eliza Miller	18
Edwin Miller	15
Charity Miller	10
Margarett Miller	8
Samuel Miller	5
Emmily Miller	3
Sarah Miller	

Father's Birthplace	Virginia	
Mother's Birthplace	Virginia	
Occupation	Keeping House	
Cannot Read	Yes	
Cannot Write	Yes	
Neighbors	View others on page	
Household Members	**Name**	**Age**
	David Miller	60
	Violet Miller	60
	Henry Miller	25
	Sam Miller	24
	Charity Miller	23
	Margaret Miller	21
	Emma Miller	11
	Sarah Miller	10
	Harrison Miller	7
	Charles Miller	3
	Margaret Miller	1
	Maggie Miller	3/12
	Mary Miller	30
	Fannie Miller	10
	William Miller	6

I had accessed the record in the National Archives database on Ancestry, marking a significant breakthrough in my search for the Un-Named. In a sea of Sarah Millers, I found the record of one who was the right age, and had at least one of the siblings that Alberta mentioned. The adults in that record were listed as David, age 60, and Violet, age 40. The ages were off but the names and relationships were right. Were David and Violet Miller the Un-Named ancestors I had been looking for?

To be sure this was the right Sarah, I needed to verify this list of siblings were indeed all the brothers and sisters of my Sarah Miller.

I needed to find this same list of Millers in another official record to be certain.

The 1880 census record, where Sarah is depicted as a 10-year-old girl, offered proof that my previous find was valid. Within this record, I could clearly see her siblings, including Harrison, whom Alberta had mentioned to me. This revelation, coupled with the knowledge that her parents were born in 1820, strongly indicated these were the right Millers. And the fact that David and Violet Miller were shown as age 60 in the 1880 census, that put their birth years as 1820 – indicating that this David and Violet Miller were slaves. The 1880 census also solidified the fact that Sarah's birthplace was the Sharswood plantation. In 1880, David and Violet are listed as farmhands.

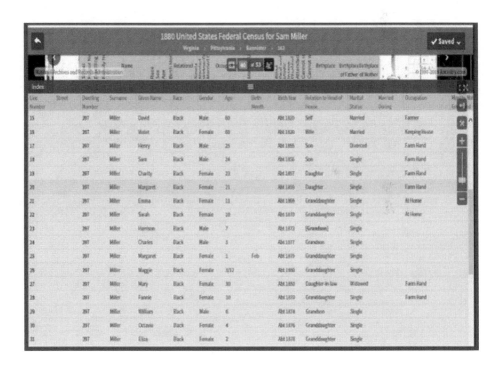

51

CERTIFICATE OF DEATH
COMMONWEALTH OF VIRGINIA
DEPARTMENT OF HEALTH, BUREAU OF VITAL STATISTICS

9187

1. PLACE OF DEATH — County: Pitts. — Registration District: Bannister

2. USUAL RESIDENCE — State: Virginia — County: Pitts.

City or Town: Java — City or Town: Java

Hospital or Institution — Rt. # 2

3. NAME OF DECEASED: Sarah Miller

4. DATE OF DEATH: April 6, 1949

5. SEX: Female — 6. COLOR OR RACE: Colored — 7. Never married

8. DATE OF BIRTH: March 10, 1868 — 9. AGE: 81

10a. USUAL OCCUPATION: Domestic — 10b. KIND OF BUSINESS: Home

11. BIRTHPLACE: Pitts. Co., Va. — 12. CITIZEN OF WHAT COUNTRY: U. S. A.

13. FATHER'S NAME: David Miller

14. MOTHER'S MAIDEN NAME: Violet Miller

19b. None

21a. ACCIDENT SUICIDE HOMICIDE: No

21d. TIME OF INJURY: None

260

22. I hereby certify that I attended the deceased from Mar. 15, 1949, to Apr 6, 1949... that death occurred at 2:30 p.m.

Signature: W. Wigington M.D. — Java, Virginia — 4-10-49

Burial — April 10, 1949 — Riceville Chyd., Riceville, Va.

4-12-49 — Mrs. W. J. Wigington

Funeral Director: Cunningham & Hughes — Geo. B. Hughes — Danville, Va.

I acquired this document during a later phase of my research, well after my initial identification of Violet and David based on oral history from Alberta. My certainty regarding the accuracy of this identification was strengthened through a cross-reference with the information concerning Violet's siblings, as provided by oral history from Alberta, and then corroborated by locating them in the census records. Given the commonality of names like Sarah and Violet Miller in Bannister County during that period, it was of utmost importance to ensure that I had correctly identified the right Sarah and Violet, which we successfully did.

Genealogy research is all about finding numerous documents and records to verify the names, dates, and familial connections of people in your tree of life. I now had firm convictions that David and Violet were the Un-Named ancestors Alberta had tasked me to find, but I kept digging, searching for even more proof. Eventually, I uncovered Sarah's death certificate, which listed her parents as David and Violet. Of course, one discovery often leads to the next journey, and I found myself interested to delve into the lives of these previously Un-Named ancestors.

Harrison Miller, the Missing Brother

The quest to research the Miller slaves commenced at the behest of Cousin Alberta, who, unfortunately, could offer no names or specific information to facilitate the search for Sarah Miller's parents. At the time, I did not have access to birth certificates through ancestry records, adding an extra layer of complexity to the challenge. I conveyed to Alberta that despite having located Sarah, the absence of her parents' names posed a substantial obstacle, and this very challenge further motivated her desire to have me embark on this search. During this research, Cousin Alberta disclosed an extraordinary revelation – the existence of Sarah's brother, Harrison. This revelation served as the pivotal clue that ultimately enabled me to unveil the identities of the enslaved individuals. The oral history passed down through the generations by Alberta Miller emerged as the linchpin in identifying these enslaved individuals. This lone clue played a critical role in definitively confirming that I had indeed identified the correct Sarah Miller within a vast database teeming with entries for individuals bearing the same name. Significantly, it was the mention of one name – "Harrison" – that illuminated the path to my connection with the Sharswood Plantation.

Harrison had mysteriously vanished without a trace. He reemerged in the family's records much later, long after Sarah had grown into adulthood. According to our family historian, there had always been lingering concerns about the fate of this missing child, as his whereabouts remained a mystery for many years. The family was perplexed as to how he could have disappeared, as he could not have been sold into slavery since he was born after the abolition of slavery.

Name	Harrison Miller
Age	24
Birth Date	Jan 1873
Birthplace	Virginia, USA
Home in 1900	Gladeville, Wise, Virginia
Sheet Number	14
Number of Dwelling in Order of Visitation	263
Family Number	275
Race	Black
Gender	Male
Relation to Head of House	Head
Marital Status	Married
Spouse's Name	Mattie Miller
Marriage Year	1893
Years Married	7
Father's Birthplace	Virginia, USA
Mother's Birthplace	Virginia, USA
Occupation	Day Laborer
Months Not Employed	1
Can Read	No
Can Write	Yes
Can Speak English	Yes
House Owned or Rented	Rent

Harrison appeared as an adult in Virginia, age 24 in the 1900 census. He's listed as a married man, married to a "Mattie Miller." This census notes that Harrison was born in 1872, seven years after slavery was abolished.

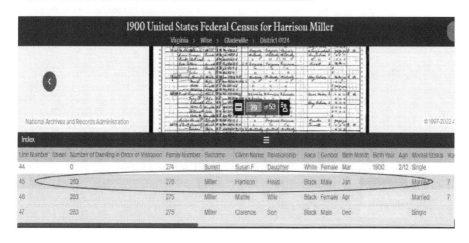

54

Violet Miller, Enslaved Woman

Drawing upon the invaluable information provided by Alberta, I embarked on a meticulous journey through historical records to trace the life of Violet. The 1880 census lists a Violet Miller who was born about 1820 and is married to a David Miller. The right names, approximate dates, and location led me to conclude this was my Violet. On March 10, 2018, a century and a half after the birth of my second great-grandmother, Sarah David Miller, who was born on March 10, 1868 at the Sharswood Plantation, I successfully identified her parents. Alberta confirmed Sarah's middle name, as it was not listed or recorded anywhere in history.

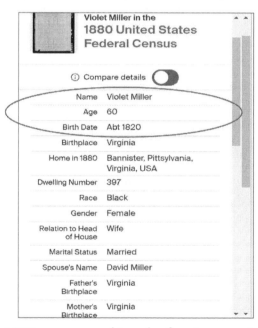

I uncovered her presence in the 1870 census data, a pivotal discovery that led me to the slaveowner Nathanial Crenshaw Miller, NC Miller. Armed with Violet's approximate age, I delved further into the past, navigating through the 1860 and 1850 slave schedules. Her age appeared to fluctuate in records, as she was classified as either 37 or 38 years old in the 1860 census. It was only in the 1870 census, marking the first instance in her entire life where she was recorded by name, that her birth year was documented as 1830. This variation in age across records is not uncommon, given the era's lack of standardized birth certificates, which often led to the misrecording of birthdates.

1870 United States Federal Census for Violet Miller

Number	Dwelling Number	Family Number	Surname	Given Name	Age	Birth Year	Gender	Race	Occupation	Real Estate Value	Personal Estate Value	Birthplace	Birth Mon
734	741		Fergerson	Ann	8	1862	Female	Black	At Home			Virginia	
734	741		Anderson	Judy	25	1845	Female	Black	Domestic Servant			Virginia	
734	741		Witcher	N W	18	1852	Male	White	Farm Laborer			Virginia	
734	741		Fergerson	Judith	40	1830	Female	White	Without Occupation			Virginia	
734	741		Barksdal	Wm L	35	1835	Male	White	Farm Laborer			Virginia	
735	742		Glap	Chas	50	1820	Male	Black	Farm Laborer			Virginia	
736	743		Logan	Anderson	60	1810	Male	Black	Farm Laborer			Virginia	
736	743		Logan	Virg	60	1810	Female	Black	Farm Laborer			Virginia	
736	743		Logan	Eliza J	18	1852	Female	Black	Farm Laborer			Virginia	
736	743		Logan	Archie	2	1868	Male	Black	At Home			Virginia	
737	744		Miller	David	60	[1810]	Male	Black	Farm Laborer			Virginia	
737	744		Miller	Violet	40	1830	Female	Black	Farm Laborer			Virginia	

My research unveiled that the Un Named Violet Miller may have come into this world at the Walnut Grove, or Cove Plantation in Halifax County, Virginia. Subsequently, she was transported to Sharswood, a location that wasn't established until 1850. Violet's birth was estimated to have occurred between 1820 and 1830. In the 1850 slave schedules, she was documented as a 28-year-old female.

"The Unveiling of our Sharswood Connection"

As I added Violet to my family tree and clicked on her name, a sense of anticipation gripped me. Then, like a bolt from the blue, a hint popped up - the 1850 census. With bated breath, I followed the link, and there it was: Violet's name in the slave schedules, owned by none other than NC Miller, situated on the Sharswood Plantation. In that moment, the weight of history crashed over me. Violet, my ancestor, a person reduced to mere property on a plantation, her identity tethered to a master's ledger. **There she was under NC Miller.** It was a stark reminder of the brutal reality faced by so many of our ancestors.

Alberta's request to uncover Violet's grandparents suddenly seemed insignificant compared to the magnitude of what I had unearthed. Sharswood wasn't just a name on a map; it was the crucible of our family's past, where generations labored under the yoke of bondage.

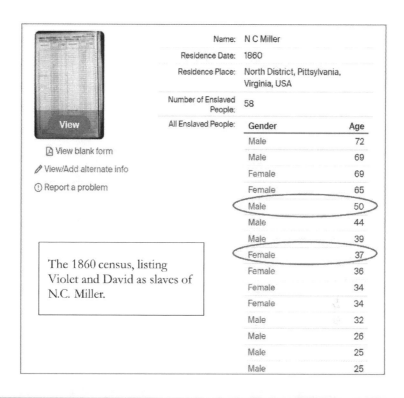

Name:	N C Miller
Residence Date:	1860
Residence Place:	North District, Pittsylvania, Virginia, USA
Number of Enslaved People:	58

All Enslaved People:

Gender	Age
Male	72
Male	69
Female	69
Female	65
Male	50
Male	44
Male	39
Female	37
Female	36
Female	34
Female	34
Male	32
Male	26
Male	25
Male	25

View

- View blank form
- View/Add alternate info
- Report a problem

The 1860 census, listing Violet and David as slaves of N.C. Miller.

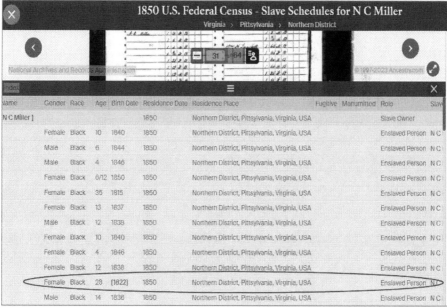

1850 U.S. Federal Census - Slave Schedules for N C Miller

Virginia > Pittsylvania > Northern District

Name	Gender	Race	Age	Birth Date	Residence Date	Residence Place	Fugitive	Manumitted	Role	Slav
N C Miller]					1850	Northern District, Pittsylvania, Virginia, USA			Slave Owner	
	Female	Black	10	1840	1850	Northern District, Pittsylvania, Virginia, USA			Enslaved Person	N C
	Male	Black	6	1844	1850	Northern District, Pittsylvania, Virginia, USA			Enslaved Person	N C
	Male	Black	4	1846	1850	Northern District, Pittsylvania, Virginia, USA			Enslaved Person	N C
	Female	Black	6/12	1850	1850	Northern District, Pittsylvania, Virginia, USA			Enslaved Person	N C
	Female	Black	35	1815	1850	Northern District, Pittsylvania, Virginia, USA			Enslaved Person	N C
	Female	Black	13	1837	1850	Northern District, Pittsylvania, Virginia, USA			Enslaved Person	N C
	Male	Black	12	1838	1850	Northern District, Pittsylvania, Virginia, USA			Enslaved Person	N C
	Female	Black	10	1840	1850	Northern District, Pittsylvania, Virginia, USA			Enslaved Person	N C
	Female	Black	4	1846	1850	Northern District, Pittsylvania, Virginia, USA			Enslaved Person	N C
	Female	Black	12	1838	1850	Northern District, Pittsylvania, Virginia, USA			Enslaved Person	N C
	Female	Black	28	[1822]	1850	Northern District, Pittsylvania, Virginia, USA			Enslaved Person	N C
	Male	Black	14	1836	1850	Northern District, Pittsylvania, Virginia, USA			Enslaved Person	N C

	in the **1850 U.S. Federal Census - Slave Schedules** ⋯			

ⓘ Compare details ◯

Gender	Female
Race	Black
Age	28
Birth Date	1822
Residence Date	1850
Residence Place	Northern District, Pittsylvania, Virginia, USA
All Enslaved People	**Name**
	N C Miller

Name:	N C Miller
Residence Date:	1850
Residence Place:	Northern District, Pittsylvania, Virginia, USA
Number of Enslaved People:	24

All Enslaved People:	Gender	Age
	Female	10
	Male	6
	Male	4
	Female	6/12
	Female	35
	Female	13
	Male	12
	Female	10
	Female	4
	Female	12
	Female	28
	Male	14
	Female	10
	Male	5
	Female	2
	Female	25

	Detail	Source
Name:	George M Y Miller	
Home in 1830 (City, County, State):	Halifax, Virginia	
Free White Persons - Males - 30 thru 39:	1	
Slaves - Males - Under 10:	1	
Slaves - Males - 10 thru 23:	6	
Slaves - Males - 24 thru 35:	1	
Free White Persons - 20 thru 49:	1	
Total Free White Persons:	1	
Total Slaves:	8	
Total - All Persons (Free White, Slaves, Free Colored):	9	

This is NC Miller's half-brother; George MY Miller. As you can see, they are from Halifax County. The Millers did not originate in Pittsylvania County, Sharswood. Their families originated from several counties in Virginia.

Violet's name was a crucial revelation, but my research unveiled that the Un-Named David Miller was documented in the 1850 slave schedules as a 45-year-old male, under the ownership of NC Miller. In the 1860 census, I also encountered an unnamed male of approximately 50 years of age, whom I believe to be David Miller. By the time of the 1870 census, he was recorded as 60 years old, this time under his given name. This progressive disclosure of their identities gradually unveiled the narrative of Violet and David Miller, shedding light on their lives as they transitioned from anonymity to being recorded by name.

The Crenshaws and the Millers

Cousin Alberta had furnished the pivotal clue that forged the connection between the Millers and Sharswood. Alberta and Grandpa Dea openly discussed the Miller family's history and the Miller plantation. Thanks to their invaluable guidance, I had managed to unearth the names of my great-great-great-grandparents. I had the privilege of sharing with Alberta the long-sought identities of her own great-grandparents, David and Violet Miller, who were once shrouded in obscurity as Un Named slaves. This significant revelation occurred before Alberta's passing in December 2019.

Based on the information gathered from Alberta, I was able to connect my unnamed ancestors, and I hungered to find out more

about where they'd lived and their lives and identities. Alberta had ties which extended deep into two prominent African American families with a significant presence in Pittsylvania County, Virginia—the Millers and the Haleys. In tracing her lineage, I uncovered the pivotal figure of Lucinda Miller, Alberta's mother, and I discovered that Lucinda's parents were Sarah P. Miller and William Crenshaw Miller.

Alberta Elizabeth Miller Womack, granddaughter of Sarah Miller.

My research revealed a fascinating twist in Alberta's family history. Another, different William

Miller, a Caucasian man, was a slave master hailing from Halifax County, Virginia. He entered into a union with the affluent Agnes Crenshaw. Their son, Nathaniel Crenshaw Miller, emerged as the original owner of the Sharswood plantation. The Crenshaws and Millers were two prosperous tobacco-growing farming families with roots spanning Hanover County, Campbell County, and Halifax, and culminating at the Sharswood Plantation in Pittsylvania County, Virginia.

What makes Alberta's family history intriguing is the peculiar nomenclature within her lineage. Her grandfather bore the name William Crenshaw Miller, representing a unique link to her ancestral past. It struck me as poetic that the very person

As the son of Sarah Miller, Nimrod "Nimmie" Miller played a significant role in shaping the family's legacy. His influence on his daughter, Alberta, was profound, instilling in her a deep appreciation for family bonds and a passion for our Miller family history.

60

who **provided the vital clues leading to the connection of my ancestors to Sharswood and the Un-Named** carried the surnames of both Crenshaw and Miller in her family heritage.

The deliberate choice of Alberta's grandfather's middle name, William Crenshaw Miller, was not a mere coincidence. It was a purposeful decision, a symbolic thread binding the past to the present. Remarkably, this naming tradition extended to Alberta's mother, Lucinda Miller, who bore the same name as a slave born in 1856.

Digging deeper into the family lineage, I uncovered the poignant fact that Alberta's grandfather, William Crenshaw Miller, was the son of slaves. It's a testament to the enduring legacy of the past, where names once stripped away were reclaimed and passed down through generations. In the case of Alberta's great-grandparents, who were initially identified as unnamed slaves, I was able to find them despite the absence of conventional names. The journey to unveil their identities may seem daunting, but it's a testament to the resilience of family historians and the determination to piece together the stories of those who were once nameless. Through diligent research and the tireless pursuit of historical records, the rich tapestry of Alberta's family history began to unfold, revealing the names and narratives that had long been hidden from view.

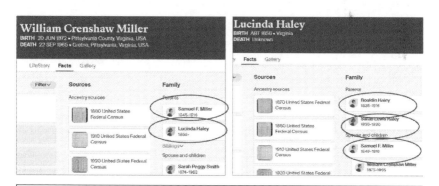

Samuel would be among the Un-Named but I have found him. Alberta's second great-grandparents on her mother Lucinda Haley's side are also found here to be amongst the Un-Named slaves. Boulden Haley and Sarah Lewis Haley are amongst the Un-Named. Alberta wanted me to only find her great-grandparents linked to Sarah Miller but instead I found them all.

My Miller Family Lineage

Through my research, I have come to understand the deep importance of Sarah's parents within the broader Miller family lineage. It appears that descendants of Sarah's mother may have been bestowed with that surname, yet many Miller descendants remained largely unaware of the true significance of this name. This lack of awareness was a direct consequence of the secrecy that shrouded the history surrounding Sarah's mother, underscoring the fact that some ancestors diligently preserved the legacy of these unnamed slaves across generations, while others did not.

The history of this Miller lineage, entwined with the lives of enslaved individuals, has remained largely unrecorded, and the profound significance of their names has gone unacknowledged, as it rightly should have been. It is an extraordinary task bestowed upon us as descendants, to piece together the intricate history of our enslaved ancestors, to honor their memory, and to acknowledge the resilience and strength they exhibited in the face of adversity.

I can vividly recall the sunlit summer day when Alberta imparted these solemn words of wisdom, to me. As I sat alongside her, she reminded me of my solemn duty to safeguard the Miller family history. I wholeheartedly embraced this responsibility. Alberta entrusted me with a sacred mission, stating, "You are now responsible for preserving our cherished Miller family history," a legacy that she had inherited from her father, Nimmie Miller. In those poignant moments, I understood the gravity of my task—to ensure that the history of Sarah Miller and her ancestors would be passed down and preserved for generations to come.

I want to inspire others to gather oral history, ancestral information and take the time to record the history and pass it down to the next generation. So many of my Miller ancestors and historians have gone on and left this earth, but they left me with the responsibility of preserving our history.

CHAPTER
FIVE

Linking the Plantation to the Un-Named

David Miller's Story

In the year 1820, a little boy is born to my unnamed ancestors. He is born a slave, ready to serve his master as his fathers have done. Young David Miller is his master's property, growing up to toil on the Plantation. My fourth great grandfather is only a child, but everyone is expected to work; there is no time to enjoy your childhood if you're a slave.

At some point, David's master Nathaniel Crenshaw Miller swaps him for another slave named "Joe" belonging to Louisa P. Miller – at least, that's what I glean from an old letter, where I learned of a slave named David. Was this my David? Could this exchange involving a David Miller between relatives possibly denote the son of my third great-grandfather? It's important to bear in mind that though slave names were consistently passed down from one generation to the next, it is unlikely that there were two slaves on the plantation bearing the same name, unless they were a father and son or otherwise closely related. So yes, I believe this *was* my David Miller, transferred as property.

A David Miller belonging to NC Miller is being exchanged between relatives. Document is dated 1859, my third great-grandfather would have been about 39 years old. This reference here is a boy David being exchanged. But note, he is listed by name. Source: Miller Papers, UNC Davis Library

Despite being removed from everything he has known, life for David continues as before, toiling for the benefit of others. Eventually David falls in love with Violet Miller, who is ten years younger than him but remains the love of his life. They might have grown up as intimate friends on the plantation, little children of the same vicinity playing together. I can only imagine the love and passion between the two love birds, based on how many children their union brings forth. By the year of the emancipation of all slaves in 1865, David and Violet Miller already had eight children and they would have two more after the Civil War ended. Violet Miller's strength to carry and nurture so many kids cannot be underestimated.

The law to free all slaves is passed in 1865 by President Abraham Lincoln. David Miller and his family live in a small slave cabin on the Sharswood plantation. They are finally freed, but now what? David and Violet have a large family to feed and can only do so if they work, and the only work they can find is to continue to serve their former master. What would a caring parent do to ensure the ability to provide for their children's needs? The couple decides there is only one choice. In the presence of God, a father takes the oath his family will continue working the land at Sharswood, this time as sharecroppers.

David and Violet Miller continue their lives in the slave cabins at the Sharswood Plantation beyond the year of emancipation. Three years after the year of emancipation, in the year 1868 when David Miller is 48 years old, my second great-grandmother is born. But Sarah Miller is born a free woman. She grew up on the Plantation, not under a slave master, but under a manager of the farm, Charles Edwin Miller. This freedom will seemingly keep her closer to her parents and siblings and grow stronger in love and family bonding. But is freedom under a former slave master actual freedom?

Document where adult David Miller signs his name with an X stating he would remain on the Sharswood Planation and work after emancipation. The year is 1868, the same year Sarah is born. Sarah would have been five months old at the time that David signed this agreement. This is proof Sarah was born and lived on this plantation now owned by her descendants. Document pulled from the Miller Papers, provided by the University of North Carolina, Davis Library.

Surviving Sharswood

For those who are not descendants of slavery, who have never endured the wrenching agony of forced removal from their homeland, who have never witnessed the heart-wrenching separation of a mother from her nursing child, and who have never experienced the cruel snatching away of a beloved partner in the dead of night, it is likely an insurmountable challenge to comprehend the profound sorrow and enduring pain of slavery.

While we may celebrate the reclamation of former slave plantation houses as an admirable achievement in preserving our history and heritage, we must pause and reflect on the human lives that were inexorably entwined with these properties. Can we fathom the unfathomable mental and emotional anguish endured by generations of Miller slaves? My ancestors, held in captivity, were under the dominion of Nathaniel Crenshaw Miller and Charles Edward Miller. Historical records attest that Nathaniel's family did, at times, free some slaves, but regrettably, none of my ancestors were among those granted their freedom. They remained against their will, bound to this plantation.

The struggles of my ancestors did not end with the abolition of slavery. These two slave masters, Nathaniel and Charles, notably never entered into marriage. One can only speculate as to why this might be, especially given their access to female slaves. After all, it was common for the census records to categorize slaves as bi-racial or mulatto, underscoring the deeply troubling dynamics that permeated Sharswood and other plantations such as those owned by the Millers and Crenshaws. Even after the official end of slavery, my ancestors remained bound to Sharswood, sentenced to a life of grueling labor for scant compensation, merely enough to sustain their existence. Consider my second great-grandmother, born on this plantation just three years after the abolition of slavery. One can only wonder about the unimaginable trials she had to endure. Although she may not have been a slave by definition, she was undeniably a victim of the enduring consequences of the institution of slavery.

The specter of the former slave master still loomed large in the lives of these freed individuals. Accounts abound of former slave owners who maintained a disturbingly active presence in the lives of their former slaves. Hidden from view, homes were built for sharecropping families far from the main roads, allowing former Caucasian slave owners to continue visiting African-American women, both married and single, long after slavery had formally ended. The grim reality was that these families had no recourse but to comply, for their very survival depended on the benevolence, or lack thereof, of the former slaveowners.

The mental trauma inflicted by slavery cast a long shadow, even after emancipation. Sarah and her family grappled with the harsh realization that their former slave masters retained control over their lives. They had no options, with nowhere to turn but to the former slaveowner or to a higher power. This was the stark reality they faced.

Sarah bore my great-grandfather Raleigh at a tender age, a circumstance that raises questions about the circumstances of her early motherhood. It is unlikely that, as a 15-year-old girl, she willingly consented to such an early motherhood. It is also telling that census records label Raleigh as mulatto, a fact which aligns with the family accounts of him passed down through generations.

The collective silence surrounding the identification of slaves within African American families can be attributed, in large part, to the enduring mental trauma inflicted by slavery. The stories handed down from generation to generation, from Violet (the slave) to Sarah (the sharecropper), detailed the relentless cruelties and unyielding hardships of slavery. Coping with this trauma meant a conscious decision to erase every painful and shameful trace of this history from their collective memory. They functioned as if it had never occurred, a defense mechanism against the transatlantic trauma they had experienced. The hushed conversations and avoidance of the topic of slavery within the African American community were methods of coping with the past, allowing them to mentally move beyond the unimaginable trauma they had endured. This silence was their way of healing from an indescribable anguish.

Linking the Plantation to Sarah and the Un-Named

There were 550,000 enslaved Black people living in Virginia in 1860, which constituted one third of the state's population. My Miller, Luck, Wimbish, Nunnally, Coles, and Womack second, third, and fourth great-grandparents were among those slaves. I have discovered my family on multiple plantations throughout rural Pittsylvania and Halifax County, Virginia, through the census records, enslaved schedules, and court records, as well as oral history records kept by my family elders that included very important names and images.

Sarah was born on the Miller plantation in 1868, but seven of her siblings were born on this plantation during slavery. Sarah's parents, my third great-grandparents, were brought to this plantation as slaves, and lived on this plantation long after slavery ended. Grandpa Dea's parents, Max Miller and Josephine Coles Miller, did not live at Sharswood but Max's parents, Charles and Rosie Miller, all worked on this plantation.

My third great-grandparents Ned and Mollie Miller were enslaved on this plantation. Parthenia Miller (b.1869), my second great-grandmother, may have also been born on this plantation. These are four distinct, different lines of Millers, *all of them are my ancestors*. I possess knowledge of their names thanks to my mother and Grandpa Dea. They provided me with the names or clues that allowed me to unravel the lineage of our Miller ancestors. And of course, it was Alberta who offered the pivotal name "Harrison" that ultimately enabled me to establish a connection with the Miller slaves, resulting in the *unequivocal link of my entire Miller family to the Sharswood Plantation*.

Despite all the family stories, I really didn't know the house down the street was in fact the same Miller Plantation of my ancestors. I was told by Grandpa Dea it was the Miller Plantation, but at the time I would never have the answers I needed to connect my family to this place. However, after I had delved so deeply into my family history, after I had come to realize just how closely we Millers were tied to the plantation, I felt the need to know indeed if my family was connected to this "Sharswood." My grandfather told the stories, but was he correct? There was no other way to find out other than to do the research.

In December of 2017, I began documenting my thoughts about how to determine if this was the origin of my family's American story. During that winter, I engaged in profound conversations with Althea, Grandpa Dea's youngest daughter. These late-night talks fortified my belief that the Sharswood house on Riceville Road was indeed the Miller Plantation.

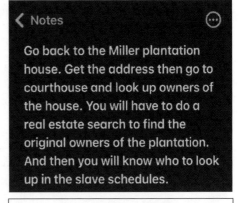

Notes from my journey to prove, one way or another, the truth of the house.

I told Althea of my intention to visit the house and uncover its history. Armed with determination, I set out to confirm the property's authenticity and, in turn, unearth the identity of the slave owner, which I hoped would lead me to our enslaved ancestors.

I embarked on this journey with no knowledge of real estate searches, relying solely on gut instinct. My first stop was the prop-

erty, where I gleaned the address from the mailbox. On December 26, 2017, I made my way to the house. Mrs. Ruby Thompson, the key to unraveling this historical mystery, was still alive. I approached the door and knocked, but there was no answer. Regardless, I snapped a photo in the waning light, listening to a feeling that this house and land were important to my story.

I proceeded to the Chatham courthouse the following week, eager to delve into the realm of real estate records. Little did I know that this property would become a focal point of my family history research, long before my cousin Frederick's purchase of Sharswood. My path had casually crossed Fred's at family reunions, but we hadn't engaged in meaningful conversations about my ongoing research; in fact, he didn't even realize that the house he had purchased had been one of my long-term research topics. In a family the size of ours, with hundreds of members living around the world, you weren't always on intimate terms with everyone. Ironically, our official introduction took place when The Washington Post expressed interest in our story, and Frederick's sister Karen reached out to me, aware of my dedication to uncovering the history of the Millers and this plantation.

My grandfather had always asserted that the Miller Plantation was "nestled in rural Pittsylvania County, Virginia." Armed with this clue, I made my way to the Pittsylvania County Courthouse. There, I meticulously traced the address back through deeds and documents, an experience that left me brimming with emotions. When I finally uncovered conclusive proof about the ownership of Sharswood, I wanted to scream even as I stood within the solemn halls of the courthouse.

Nathaniel Crenshaw Miller of Sharswood

At the courthouse, I uncovered that the original owner of the Miller Plantation was Nathaniel Crenshaw Miller. His Crenshaw family was easy to discover. The ancestors pertinent to my research are Charles Crenshaw (fl. 1775–1794) who married Sarah Bacon (d. 1818) and lived in Hanover County. Charles and Sarah had six children. Their daughter Agnes married William Miller of Halifax County. Agnes and William had a son in 1816 they named Nathaniel Crenshaw Miller (1816–1888) – the man who would eventually become the slaveowner of my Miller ancestors. William Miller also had another son, George Y. M. Miller (fl. 1826–1863), by a previous marriage. George is Charles Edwin Miller's father, and his mother was Laura M. Miller.

Agnes and William's son Nathaniel remained a bachelor, as did their grandson, Charles Edwin Miller (1839–1906). Neither married or have legitimate children that we know of. Nathaniel was gifted Sharswood by his parents; it is Nathaniel who enslaved my ancestors David and Violet Miller, as evidenced by the 1850 census noting a "28-year-old black female" listed under "N.C. Miller."

in the

•••

1850 U.S. Federal Census - Slave Schedules

ⓘ Compare details

Gender	Female
Race	Black
Age	28
Birth Date	1822
Residence Date	1850
Residence Place	Northern District, Pittsylvania, Virginia, USA
All Enslaved People	**Name**
	N C Miller

The 1860 census, listing Violet and David as slaves of N.C. Miller.

Name:	George M Y Miller
Home in 1830 (City, County, State):	Halifax, Virginia
Free White Persons - Males - 30 thru 39:	1
Slaves - Males - Under 10:	1
Slaves - Males - 10 thru 23:	6
Slaves - Males - 24 thru 35:	1
Free White Persons - 20 thru 49:	1
Total Free White Persons:	1
Total Slaves:	8
Total - All Persons (Free White, Slaves, Free Colored):	9

This is NC Miller's half-brother George They are from Halifax County. The Millers did not originate in Pittsylvania County, Sharswood. Their families originated from several counties in Virginia.

Researching the Records – Again

The land we now know as Sharswood was part of a crown grant for 2,400 acres to the Crenshaw family in 1820, and they sold it to William Miller that same year for 2,000 pounds. Sharswood was deeded to Nathaniel Crenshaw Miller by his father William Miller in 1838. The house later passed to Charles E. Miller and then later to Charles Miller's nephews Fred and Will Davis.

According to a descendant of the Caucasian Crenshaws, the family originally hailed from Crenshaw, Mississippi. While I had intended to meet with this descendant, I regrettably did not do so before completing this book.

Date
1751
Land Survey (Pittsylvania Co. Va)
This land was afterword acquired
by the Crenshaw family, descending
to the Millers.
(Note looking of newspaper of prerevolution
days) Thos. Fredrix Davis

A document held at the University of North Carolina confirms how NC Miller's family (the Crenshaw line) acquired the land from his wealthy parents.

Armed with the knowledge that N.C. Miller and Charles Edwin Miller were the original proprietors of the Miller Plantation, I logged into my Ancestry.com account and embarked on my quest to locate these slaveholders. I shall forever remember that date – February 24, 2018 – the day when I unearthed the 1870 census records documenting the original slaveowners of the Miller Plantation. Only one month later, I would learn the identity of the slaves.

1870 United States Federal Census Census			
	Name:	Chas E Miller	Feb 23, 2018
	Age in 1870:	27	
	Birth Date:	abt 1843	
	Birthplace:	Virginia	
	Dwelling Number:	2767	
	Home in 1870:	Subdivision North of Dan River, Pittsylvania, Virginia	
	Race:	White	
	Gender:	Male	
	Post Office:	Chatham	
	Occupation:	Manager At Farm	
	Male Citizen Over 21:	Yes	
	Inferred Father:	N C Miller	
	Household Members:	6	

Charles Miller is listed in the 1870 census as "Chas E Miller" – yet another example of imprecise naming in official records. This gave me another name to use in my records searches, and was the key to connecting the house on Riceville Road to the Caucasian Miller family. As I looked through deeds and property documents, I found a property survey plat for the house which clearly designated the property as Sharswood. Imagine my joy when I noticed "Chas E. Miller" listed with a flourish as the owner. It was my undeniable confirmation; the moment I realized I had unequivocally located the Miller plantation.

The plat, which clearly designates the property as Sharswood, with a particularly crucial detail: Chas E. Miller listed as the owner in the upper right.

Lastly, I lend to my beloved wife Sarah, the whole of my Estate real & personal not already given away during her life, to be Equally divided at her death among my children, or given up to them as she may think proper during her life. Having regard to those stocks &c that have been already given up by me.

My Will is, that there be no inventory or appraisement made of my estate.

I appoint my sons John Crenshaw, Nathaniel Crenshaw and Charles Crenshaw, Executors of this my last Will & Testament.

Given under my hand & Seal this 9th day of Feby. one thousand seven hundred & ninety.

Last Will & Testament of Charles Crenshaw dated 1 May 1820

The following I make my last Will & Testament respecting my Property

Viz. Imprimis - That my negroes including those left me by my Sister shall be provided for by emancipation, when the Law will admit of it in a way consistent with their happiness. Until this can be done, that they be Kept together upon my Plantations & treated as well as their situation will admit of, subject to such regulations as may be necessary to keep them regularly employed. Such proportion of the proceeds of their labour as may be fairly due for their services after a moderate allowance for the use of the land &c. to be applied to their present use, & to constitute a fund for their future accommodation. The balance of my Estate to be equally divided among my Sister Miller's Children & my Niece Mary B. Rice & my Nephew Izard B. Rice. Under this devise it is to be understood that my Land is to be reserved till the negroes can be better provided for than by being Kept together on it. Should any misfortune, by failure of Crops or of a market for them, happens, so as to produce a deficiency for the comfortable subsistence of the negroes, it must be supplied out of the rest of my Estate. Then after this object is affected, The Children of my Sister Agnes Miller & my niece Mary B. Rice & Izard B. Rice are to inherit my property equally they & their Heirs forever Viz, they, or the Survivors of them & their Heirs forever.

Finally I appoint as Executors of this my last Will my Brother in law Wm Miller & my Neighbor Martin Strong— Wishing no appraisement of my Property &

In a will dated 1820, Nathaniel Crenshaw Miller's mother, Agnes, is listed as one of the beneficiaries. His father, William Miller, is designated as both a brother-in-law and an executor. An interesting note in the will emphasizes the importance of keeping enslaved individuals together on the land. This particular provision might shed light on why David and Violet, along with their families, were permitted to remain together throughout the period of slavery. Moreover, my research has uncovered other ancestors from this plantation who were allowed to enter into matrimony and raise children.

I had the correct property – now I needed to trace it as it changed hands through the years. I immersed myself deeply in the deeds, meticulously poring over each ownership record as the land was split into smaller and smaller parcels and sold off. As I approached the records pertaining to Sharswood's proprietors, a surge of emotions overcame me, erupting like a long-dormant volcano. This experience was profound, akin to finally closing the chapter on my elusive family history. These individuals had attempted to obscure my heritage, keeping it out of the educational curriculum, be it about the South, the county, or the plantation. Yet, through the power of oral history and technology, I managed to unveil it all. The information I sought was right there, intricately woven among several landowners. Notably, the land had once been in the possession of the very slave owner who held the key to my past.

1913 deed splitting the land into three plots.

THIS DEED made this 29th day of December 1913, between S. F. Davis and Annie C. Davis, his wife, parties of the first part, James L. Tredway and Almeyda Tredway, his wife, parties of the second part and A. C. Brown and Edwin S. Reid, parties of the third part.

WITNESSETH That whereas the said parties of the first part were the owners of the tract of land herinafter described and conveyed and whereas they sold said tract of land to the aforesaid James L. Tredway, one of the parties of the second part and whereas, before the purchase money was all paid, the said James L. Tredway sold the said tract of land to the said parties of the third part, for the sum of seventeen thousand dollars and whereas the said James L. Tredway has paid to the said S. F. Davis the whole amount of the purchase money due him on said land, before the execution and delivery of this deed, the receipt thereof is hereby acknowledged, and whereas the said parties of the third part have before the execution and delivery of this deed paid to the said parties of the second part, the said sum of seventeen thousand dollars, in full for said purchase money for said land due him, the receipt whereof is hereby acknowledged, and whereas, the said parties of the second part have requested and directed the said parties of the first part to convey the said land to the said parties of the third part as is evidenced by their uniting in this deed. Now, therefore, the said parties of the first and second parts, for and in consideration of the payment of the said sum of seventeen thousand dollars, of which the said parties of the first part have received the amount due them on said land and the said parties of the second part have received the residue thereof, the receipt whereof is hereby acknowledged, do hereby give, grant, bargain, sell and convey to the said parties of the third part, with general warranty of title, all that certain tract of land lying and being in the County of Pittsylvania, Virginia, on the waters of Stinking River at and near Mount Airs adjoining the

78

Surveyor, in the year 1874, to which reference is hereby made, for a more particular description of it, but from said tract of land there is to be deducted a certain tract of land lying on the extreme South West corner of said tract, known as the Clark's mill tract, containing eighty and ⁷⁵/100 acres, which has been conveyed by S. H. Davis and wife by deed dated 11ᵗʰ day of December 1913, to Sallie Dodd and Louisa Miller and recorded in the Clerk's Office of the Circuit Court of Pittsylvania County, in Deed Book 142 at page 416, to which reference is hereby made. And it is further covenanted and agreed, that the said parties of the second and third parts assume the payment of the annuity placed on said land of one hundred dollars per annum, to Mrs. Ellen Sarr, during her life and, at her death to her daughter Miss Laura Sarr, during her life, and which annuities are hereby made a lien on all of the said land as specified under the said will and testament of Charles E. Miller, deceased and which is to remain and continue a lien on all of said land, until fully paid. Witness our hands and seals.

S. H. Davis   [Sea]
Annie C. Davis   [Sea]
James L. Tredway   [Sea]
Almeyda Tredway   [Sea]

Lot No. 20 originally containing 163-1/2 acres, more or less, but from which there is to be deducted 5 acres, more or less, previously conveyed to the party of the second part by the parties of the first part by deed dated May 4, 1961 and recorded in the Clerk's Office of the Circuit Court of Pittsylvania County in Deed Book 409, at page 94; Lot No. 21 containing 44-8/10 acres, more or less, and Lot No. 22 containing 37 4/10 acres, more or less, according to map of D. T. Williams, C. E. recorded in the Clerk's Office of the Circuit Court of Pittsylvania County, Virginia, in Deed Book No. 143, at page 234, and being the same property conveyed to J. A. Thompson by E. S. Reid and Frances T. Reid, his wife, by deed dated July 12, 1917, and recorded in said Clerk's Office in Deed Book 153, at page 183, to which map and deed reference is hereby made for a more particular description of said land.

E.S. Reid sells property to J.A. Thompson for $5,850 in a deed dated July 12, 1917.

The deeds unequivocally established Charles Edwin Miller as the proprietor of Sharswood. Inside that courthouse, an overwhelming sense of validation washed over me. I had an urge to let out a triumphant scream, but I held it in. Instead, the words kept repeating in my mind: "Dea was right. He was absolutely right." Throughout the years, my grandfather had steadfastly maintained that the place we knew on Riceville Road as the Miller Plantation was indeed Sharswood. And now, with the deed as my testament, I had undeniable proof. Grandpa Dea had gifted me the clues, the knowledge, and the rich history I needed to confirm that this hallowed ground was the birthplace of my ancestors.

Owners of Sharswood

Courthouse documents showed the Crenshaw Family having passed the Sharswood land to the Millers of Halifax County, Virginia. The land was passed to William Miller. William married Agnes Crenshaw, hence the transfer of land from the Crenshaws to the Millers. Structure number one having been built prior to 1850, a deed says 1820.

According to a descendant owner of the Sharswood plantation, the initial structure was erected earlier, but unfortunately succumbed to flames during a **slave rebellion**. The house acquired by Fred stands as the plantation's second structure built in 1850.

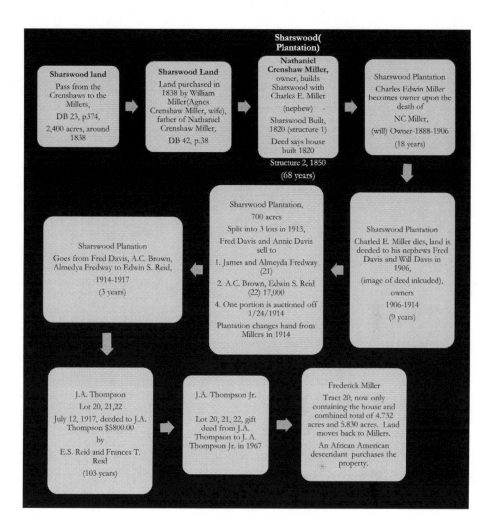

Sharswood(Plantation)

Sharswood land
Pass from the Crenshaws to the Millers,
DB 23, p374,
2,400 acres, around 1838

Sharswood Land
Land purchased in 1838 by William Miller(Agnes Crenshaw Miller, wife), father of Nathaniel Crenshaw Miller,
DB 42, p.38

Nathaniel Crenshaw Miller,
owner, builds Sharswood with Charles E. Miller
(nephew)
Sharswood Built, 1820 (structure 1)
Deed says house built 1820
Structure 2, 1850
(68 years)

Sharswood Plantation
Charles Edwin Miller becomes owner upon the death of
NC Miller,
(will) Owner-1888-1906
(18 years)

Sharswood Planation
Goes from Fred Davis, A.C. Brown, Almedya Fredway to Edwin S. Reid,
1914-1917
(3 years)

Sharswood Plantation,
700 acres
Split into 3 lots in 1913,
Fred Davis and Annie Davis sell to
1. James and Almeyda Fredway (21)
2. A.C. Brown, Edwin S. Reid (22) 17,000
4. One portion is auctioned off 1/24/1914
Plantation changes hand from Millers in 1914

Sharswood Plantation
Charled E. Miller dies, land is deeded to his nephews Fred Davis and Will Davis in 1906,
(image of deed inlcuded),
owners
1906-1914
(9 years)

J.A. Thompson
Lot 20, 21,22
July 12, 1917, deeded to J.A. Thompson $5800.00
by
E.S. Reid and Frances T. Reid
(103 years)

J.A. Thompson Jr.
Lot 20, 21, 22, gift deed from J.A. Thompson to J. A. Thompson Jr. in 1967

Frederick Miller
Tract 20, now only containing the house and combined total of 4.732 acres and 5.830 acres. Land moves back to Millers.
An African American descendant purchases the property.

1. William deeds the land to his son Nathaniel Crenshaw Miller 1838, he builds Sharswood, 1850. A local historian claims that the original building was destroyed in a fire caused by a slave rebellion.
2. NC Miller dies and leaves the land to a "Chas E Miller", or Charles Edwin Miller in 1888
3. Charles Edwin Miller, has the plantation 18 years from 1888-1906
4. 1906 Charles Edwin Miller dies, and the land is deeded to his nephews Fred and Will Davis, Fred and Will are the sons of NC Miller's sister Park Miller Davis.

5. Deed dated December 29, 1913, showing the split up of Sharswood into 3 parcels of land. The agreement is being negotiated with Fred Davis (Annie Davis, wife). In this document it looks as if they are the owners, and are selling off portions of land which includes lot 20 which is the portion that Frederick Miller now owns. Deeds show that Fred Davis is now the sole owner.

6. The names on the second portion of land are James and Almeyda Fredway. (no longer owned by Miller family)

7. The third portion of land will now be owned by A.C. Brown and Edwin S. Reid who purchased the third part. (The land is no longer owned by the Miller family)

8. Another eighty acres of land was conveyed to Sallie Dodd and Louisa Miller by Fred Davis. It looks as if he is selling off the estate. Louisa Miller was in a previous document swapping slaves with Nathaniel Crenshaw Miller. Deedbook 425, pg. 495

9. JA Thompson was conveyed the land on July 12, 1917, he did not purchase it from the original slave owners. He purchased the land from Edwin S. Reid.

10. In May 2020, 152 years after Sarah's birth on the Sharswood Plantation, her great-grandson Fred Miller purchased the land from Kathleen Thompson Puckett. Fred's ownership now marks him as the first African American owner of the Miller Plantation.

The African American Connection to the Caucasian Millers

Because slaves often used the surnames of their slavemasters, there are two family lines of Millers in this area of Virginia, divided by ethnicity. The Caucasian Millers came to the Sharswood plantation from Halifax County, Virginia. In 1840 George YM Miller, who is Nathaniel Crenshaw Miller's half-brother, owned 34 slaves on his farm in Halifax (according to the census). In 1850 George owned 38 slaves, but by 1860, he only had 6. This may have been because of shifting his slave labor to the new plantation called Sharswood purchased by William Miller and Agnes Crenshaw Miller for their son Nathaniel; the 1860 census places George in Pittsylvania County, Virginia.

Birthplace	Virginia
Home in 1850	Northern District, Halifax, Virginia, USA
Occupation	Farmer
Industry	Agriculture
Real Estate	20000
Line Number	38
Dwelling Number	724
Family Number	727
Inferred Spouse	Laura Miller
Inferred Child	Ellen Miller; William Miller; Thomas S Miller; Charles E Miller; Ann P Miller

Household members

Name	Age
George M S Miller	53
Laura Miller	34
Ellen Miller	15
William Miller	13
Thomas S Miller	12
Charles E Miller	10
Ann P Miller	8

Name	Ges M Y Miller [George Mercer Yuille Miller]
Age	65
Birth Year	abt 1795
Gender	Male
Race	White
Birth Place	Virginia
Home in 1860	North District, Pittsylvania, Virginia

The 1850 census record for George Miller lists his home as Halifax County.

By the 1860 census, George has moved to Pittsylvania County.

By 1860, ten years after Sharswood has been established, Nathaniel Crenshaw Miller is the owner of the plantation and is recorded as having 58 slaves. George was getting older, and thus his younger half-brother took over the tobacco farming at Sharswood. That is why the bulk of the slaves and the slave trade for the Miller clan had been transferred from Halifax County to the huge Sharswood plantation in Pittsylvania County.

The 1860 census is also of interest because of what it tells us about the Crenshaw family. NC Miller's great-grandfather, was part of the prosperous Crenshaw family, originating from Hanover County, Virginia. Hanover County contains the city of Richmond,

Detail Source

Name:	N C Miller [Nathaniel Crenshaw Miller]
Age:	44
Birth Year:	abt 1816
Gender:	Male
Birth Place:	Virginia
Home in 1860:	North District, Pittsylvania, Virginia
Post Office:	Riceville
Dwelling Number:	1255
Family Number:	1255
Occupation:	Farmer
Real Estate Value:	30000
Personal Estate Value:	80000

Household Members	Age
N C Miller	44
Ges M Y Miller	65
N B Miller	23

In the 1860 census, Nathanial is living in Pittsylvania County, Virginia, and is noted as the head of the household, with his brother George ("Ges M Y Miller") living with him.

83

which is the place my ancestors initially arrived at on slave ships from Africa. It is likely some of my Un-Named ancestors were purchased by Nathaniel Crenshaw and listed in his 1860 census.

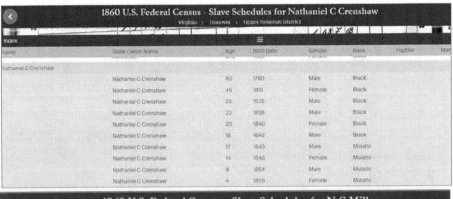

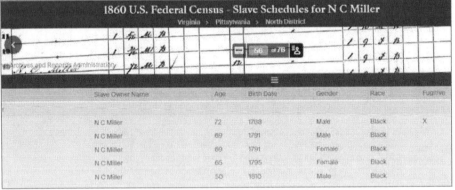

I believe the 50-year-old male born in 1810 is my third great-grandfather David, based on his age in the 1870 census where he is listed by name.

Just prior to the Civil War in 1861, as the Miller family was shifting their farm from Halifax County to Pittsylvania County, there was a movement in America known as the "Back-to-Africa" movement. Championed by the American Colonization Society, this social movement advocated resettling American-born blacks in Africa. Both abolitionists and slave owners supported this idea. Abolitionists wanted to free African slaves and their descendants, and providing them with the opportunity to return to Africa and their erstwhile cultures. Slave owners also wanted to send freed African Americans back to Africa, but for a less altruistic reason – they believed free blacks endangered the system of slavery by showing enslaved people what was possible as a freedman.

It is uncertain whether the Crenshaws were actual members of the American Colonization Society. But we do know that in 1853, Nathaniel Crenshaw repatriated one of his slaves back to Africa. Specifically, we see that he returned a 21-year-old man to Liberia after granting him freedom.

8,041 emigrants sent to Liberia

Nathaniel C Crenshaw, the 2nd great grandfather to Nathaniel Crenshaw Miller sends a slave back to Africa in 1853

In this proclamation, there is a mention of a program that involved repatriating slaves to Africa. It seems Nathaniel Crenshaw, who is the great grandfather of Nathaniel Crenshaw Miller participated in a repatriation program.

This man, Gilbert Austin, was part of a group of African Americans who embarked on the Ship Banshee from two different locations. The first group departed from Baltimore, Maryland on November 9, 1853, while the second group left from Norfolk, Virginia on November 11, 1853. (Interestingly, among the passengers on this ship were also five members of the Burke family, who had been emancipated by Robert E. Lee.) This voyage was organized by members of the American Colonization Society, with Captain Wingate serving as the Ship Master. This is a copy of the relevant portion of this manifest.

164	Dabney Morris	24	"	"
165	Lucy Morris	20	"	"
166	Rosabella Morris	1	"	"
167	Gilbert Austin	21	"	Em. by Nathaniel C. Crenshaw
	Nottoway Co., VA			
168	Edmund Jones	21	Slave	Em. by Mrs. C Jones
189	Isabella Brown	4 mos	"	
	Vincennes, Indiana			
190	Cornelius Simms	49	Slave	Em. by Indiana becoming a Free State
191	Elizabeth Simms	33	Free	
192	Charles Simms	18	"	
193	William Simms	14	"	
194	Sarah Simms	12	"	
195	George W. Simms	10	"	
196	Charlotte Simms	6	"	
197	Thomas Simms	4	"	
	Princeton, Indiana			
198	Jacob Stephenson	56	Slave	Em. by Mrs. Stephenson of South Carolina
199	Harrison Stephenson	14	"	Em. by D. R. Stephenson of S.C
200	Robert Stephenson	12	"	"
201	Charles Stephenson	10	"	"
202	James W. Stephenson	8	"	"
	Madison, Indiana			
203	Rev. John McKey	39	Slave	Purchased himself
	Wayne County, Indiana			
204	David Matthews	37	Free	
205	Alley Matthews	28	"	
206	William H. Matthews	12	"	
207	Frederick Matthews	7	"	
208	David Matthews	2	"	
	Fayette County, Kentucky			

Charles Edwin Miller

Image of Charles Edwin Miller, Sharswood Slaveowner. Credit: Library of Virginia ⁓Originial Author: Foster's Photographic, Gallery, Richmond, Virginia: 1901. Charles was a member of The Constitutional Convention of Virginia from 1901-1902.

MEMBERS AND OFFICERS OF
The Constitutional Convention of Virginia,
RICHMOND—1901-'2.

87

While it is admirable that Nathaniel Crenshaw allowed one man to return to the land of his ancestors, he still continued to own a plantation full of enslaved people. As mentioned, when his daughter Agnes married William Miller and later purchased Sharswood, that farm was also run by slave labor. And on plantations as large as those owned by the Miller and Crenshaw families, the daily work of slaves was directed by an overseer. Brice Barksdale was the overseer of slaves at the Sharswood Plantation until his passing in 1846. Following Brice, his brother-in-law Draper Hancock assumed the role of overseer. John J. Barksdale, Brice's son, held the position of overseer on the Miller plantation after his uncle.

In the post-slavery era, John Barksdale's mother, Matilda Barksdale, played a significant role in the community by providing land for a black school and the black church known as Mount Airy. My Sarah Miller attended the Mount Airy school and was an active member of this church. It's likely that her children also received their education at the black school associated with Mount Airy. While the school is no longer standing, the church is still there and plays an active role in the community.

John J. Barksdale, overseer on the Miller plantation.

Photo courtesy of Aubrey Bennett, John's great-grandson

As the nineteenth century turned into the twentieth, Charles Miller contributed to the board of trustee potentially assisting in the construction of schools and churches for former slaves, underscoring his dedication to their progress. Nevertheless, his trajectory shifted notably when he participated as a delegate in the Virginia Constitutional Convention of 1901-02. Throughout this time, he ardently advocated for the implementation of poll taxes, as well as literacy and comprehension criteria for voting. Sadly, these measures had the detrimental effect of severely limiting the electorate, swiftly disenfranchising African Americans.

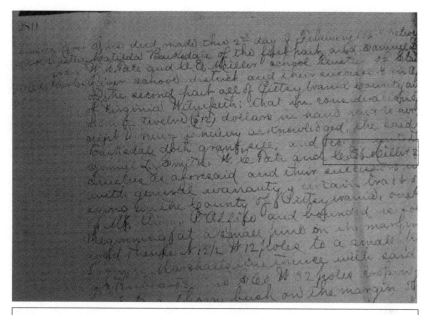

Deed showing Mount Airy School in which Charles Miller was a trustee after slavery. According to a local historian, Charles assisted with establishing a church and a school for the former enslaved.

Connecting African Millers to Nathaniel Crenshaw Miller?

In the course of my research, I had the unique opportunity to meet a direct descendant of the Miller family, namely the grand-daughter of Stonewall Jackson Miller. Mrs. Ruby Robinson, a resident of Los Angeles, who at the time was 80 years old, graciously shared her invaluable insights. It is noteworthy that Mrs. Robinson had previously been interviewed by Anita McGee Royston, the editor of the book titled "Our Black Mothers." In these interviews, she had candidly recounted her personal experiences and offered her profound knowledge about her upbringing and the rich history of Pittsylvania County, Virginia.

Stonewall Jackson Miller and his descendants are recognized for their notably fair complexion. In historical records, they are some-times documented as "Caucasian." Following a discussion with Mrs. Robinson, she affirmed the physical attributes of her ancestors, and

I also was able to view images of her family members who, unquestionably, could easily "pass" as white. During our conversation, I specifically inquired with Mrs. Robinson about the oral history concerning her grandparents and whether they were once enslaved.

What is particularly intriguing from our discussions is that Mrs. Robinson, who had personal knowledge of her grandmother, could not recall anyone mentioning that her grandparents had ever been enslaved. Moreover, her grandmother, whom she had met, never indicated that she had experienced slavery. The research indicates a potential genetic connection between this branch of the Millers and the Caucasian Millers of Sharswood. Mrs. Robinson's second great-grandfather was indeed enslaved;however, he is recorded as "mulatto." Through my investigation, I have uncovered evidence of Mrs. Ruby's third great-grandfather, whom I believe to be a Caucasian Miller. The individual under scrutiny is identified as John Miller, and there's a potential connection to the Sharswood Millers. I'm currently immersed in further research to gather compelling evidence in support of this hypothesis. It seems that John Miller fathered a son named Pauldo, occasionally noted as Paul, who was born around 1841 and lived in slavery. Paul is the lone enslaved person within the Miller lineage whom I could trace back to the Caucasian Millers. Interestingly, I uncovered Pauldo's existence only after consulting with Miller family historians, including Mrs. Ruby Robinson and another lifelong resident and educator of Pittsylvania County, who happened to be a direct descendant of Pauldo. Adding to the intrigue of this discovery is that my grandmother, Anglean Miller, had previously hinted at our ties to this lineage of Black Millers before I embarked on this investigation. The Caucasian Millers and African American Millers coexisted with-out delving into the sensitive topic of slavery. This situation may offer an explanation for the presence of a slave burial ground with my ancestors, a discovery that had remained concealed from my African American Miller family.

Name	Pauldo Miller
Gender	Male
Race	Black
Death Age	85
Birth Date	abt 1836
Death Date	17 Jan 1921
Death Place	Pittsylvania, Virginia, USA
Registration Date	7 Jul 1921
Father	John Miller

CHAPTER
SIX

My Past, My Present

Stepping on Sacred Ground

All of this information about the Millers, the Crenshaws, the Un-Named, and the Plantation itself – all of it was research I was pursuing to further my own understanding of my tree of life. I had spoken to some family members about it, those who I eagerly begged for stories and information, hoping to glean additional clues with each retelling. But my family is large, and as with any large family, not all members are close.

So, in May of 2020, when my cousin Frederick Miller assumed ownership of a house on Riceville Road, he could not have known I was already looking into the history of the property. His primary goal was to secure a place that could become the cherished venue for our enduring annual Hamm-Coles family reunion, a tradition deeply embedded in our family's heritage for over five decades. When the opportunity to purchase the spacious house on ten acres of land presented itself, he eagerly embraced it. At that time, the 1850s house appeared to him as a tranquil countryside residence set on a serene piece of land. Initially, Fred and his family were unaware of the house's historical significance or the stories of its previous inhabitants.

Following Fredrick Miller's acquisition of Sharswood, I received an invitation to visit the estate from his sister, Karen Dixon-Rexroth. Over the subsequent months, Karen and I engaged in frequent discussions, delving deeply into my research findings regarding the Miller family's history, the lives of David and Violet, and the ownership of the plantation.

The Washington Post Article

In 2021, when the Washington Post began a story on Sharswood, Karen referred the reporter to me to delve into Sarah Miller's family history, which is how I became involved in the story. It's important to emphasize that I had already identified David and Violet, the slaves back in 2018, using information I had gathered from Alberta Miller Womack. Subsequently, I shared these discoveries with Karen, who, in turn, relayed them to a local genealogist. The primary objective was to engage the genealogist in uncovering further information regarding the connection between the plantation and our enslaved ancestors.

Throughout my journey to unlock the secrets of my tree of life, my ancestors have called out to me, urging me to acknowledge their existence and find them in the annals of history. I have felt their guidance in the chance conversations which revealed long-sought clues as I've poured through records both digital and paper. The discovery of a Miller slave burial ground during the filming of 60 Minutes was no coincidence; it felt like destiny, marking the concluding chapter in my eleven-year quest to locate Sarah and my elusive ancestors, the Un-Named.

In memory of my departed cousin, C.D. Hamm. C.D. and his family played a pivotal role in preserving this cherished tradition for over half a century. I can vividly recall a moment at one of our family reunions when he turned to me and proposed a question, "Why don't all of you who've received a college education return here and construct a facility in Cody for our gatherings? We truly need a dedicated venue for our family reunions." Fortunately, Fred secured Sharswood for our family gatherings.

Stepping onto the soil for the very first time where my enslaved ancestors once walked upon was a remarkably moving experience, one that evoked a mixture of emotions. The weight of history, suffering, resilience, and the enduring legacy of those who had toiled on this land for generations was palpable. It was a poignant reminder of the injustices of the past and the long journey towards progress and understanding. Standing on that hallowed ground, I felt a deep connection to my heritage and an unwavering commitment to preserving and sharing the stories of those who had endured the hardships of slavery. It was a moment that highlighted the importance of acknowledging our history, both its triumphs and its darkest chapters, and of ensuring that the legacy of those who walked that soil lives on, honored and remembered.

In this moment, I find myself gazing down at the very earth that once bore witness to the presence of my enslaved ancestors, David and Violet, as well as my second great-grandmother, Sarah Miller, all of whom resided on the Sharswood Plantation. I needed a moment to absorb it all.

60 Minutes to Change a Life

The first I heard of 60 Minutes' interest in my family's story was when a producer reached out to me through Facebook, expressing a keen interest in featuring us on their program. I facilitated the connection between the producer and my cousin Karen Dixon-Rexroth, which ultimately led to the unfolding of the 60 Minutes story. It was an honor to discuss my research, and the arrival of an entire film crew at my home was a life-changing experience.

During their visit to Gretna, Virginia, the crew captured footage at several locations, but one place left an indelible mark on me. On a cold and rainy February day, I drove to Sharswood to meet with the production crew. I felt most comfortable in the company of my cousin Dexter Miller, given his deep knowledge of our Miller family history. Dexter and I had embarked on rides together in the past, so when he suggested we take a ride with the 60 Minutes film crew, it didn't seem unusual. However, on that day, Dexter chose to keep the destination a secret.

Upon arrival at a private home, I stepped out of Dexter's truck and found myself standing before an open plot of land adjacent to the nearby home. The property owner warmly greeted us, and Dexter introduced me as his cousin. The owner then pointed to a specific area, and we made our way to this significant location. Together, we took a few steps towards what appeared to be an unassuming site.

To my astonishment, it became apparent that we were standing on the grounds of a slave burial site no more than ten minutes from Sharswood. As we approached the burial ground, I couldn't help but slow down, trying to absorb the gravity of the moment. It was a mixture of disbelief and overwhelming emotion. As I walked around the area, the unmarked stones stood in silent testimony to the countless unnamed individuals laid to rest there. Rows of these stones, possibly a hundred or more,

The Miller slave cemetery.

Photo by Sonya Womack Miranda

stretched before me. Some were large, while others were smaller, likely representing children or infants. Not a single one of these stones bore the name of my ancestors.

My ancestors had been laid to rest with simple stone markers in the ground, devoid of birth or death dates. For centuries, they went unrecognized and unacknowledged. Their existence remained a hidden chapter in history. But on February 13, 2022, as I walked amidst their sacred burial ground, an emotional connection transcended time and space. The enslaved souls buried there seemed to cry out in unison, and in that moment, a clear sunny day unexpectedly transformed into a snowy spectacle. The snowflakes were their tears, conveying, "You found us, you found us! Thank God, you have found us."

These ancestors toiled relentlessly in the tobacco fields of Nathaniel Crenshaw Miller's plantation, nurturing dreams of a better life for their children and themselves. I, Sonya Womack-Miranda, their Miller descendant, am convinced that I am the living embodiment of their dreams and hopes. I accept the responsibility of owning their history and sharing their story, one that focuses not on the slave master, but on the slaves themselves. No longer will they remain among the Un-Named.

As I reflect on that moment, it still feels like a blur, an unexpected turn in my quest. I had no idea how I had arrived at the burial grounds of my ancestors, just minutes away from the Sharswood plantation. I wondered if anyone else who had visited this site had truly grasped the significance of what lay before us. It struck me that these individuals had not been deemed worthy of even having their names recorded for future identification or family remembrance. In that moment, I longed for solitude with my ancestors, to fully absorb and process the profound experience unfolding before me. I cannot adequately express the depth of my emotions during this experience. I walked amidst those unmarked graves, contemplating the identities of those who rested there. My fourth or fifth great-grandparents were among them, and I had finally returned to them. How could they have known? On that day, the sky above remained a crystal-clear blue, but as soon as I stepped onto the burial site, it began to snow. It was as if they were saying, "You have come home. You have found us, even if we have no names to identify us."

These unadorned stones that serve as silent sentinels mark the very souls of my ancestors now at rest. They lie here, untouched by any name or record, deliberately hidden from my knowledge and my family. Yet, the connection I share with them binds our souls, and in that connection, I find a meaningful sense of belonging to something greater than myself. I found it ironic that the first two African Americans to set foot on this land was Dexter and myself who were both descendants of the very slaves whose history was enshrined in that sacred place. It was as if this encounter had been orchestrated by a higher power, perhaps even by God Himself.

The connection to this place filled a void in me. Previously, I often felt incomplete, but now, I was at peace, knowing another part of my family legacy. Witnessing the burial ground, Sarah's house, touching the slave cabin, and feeling the walls of the slave castles in Africa, and learning the names of my enslaved ancestors - it all felt like my entire life had come full-circle in that moment.

In a cruel twist of fate, my enslaved "Un-Named" ancestors tasted the bitter fruit of freedom during their lives, only to find their eternal rest upon the very soil that once held them in bondage. The irony of Fred Miller, their descendant, now owning the plantation where his great-greatgrandparents are laid to rest, is beyond comprehension.

David Miller lived out his days in solitary existence as a widower in a rooming house, suggesting that Violet was likely the first to depart this world. The Sharswood Plantation stands today as a solemn monument to their tumultuous journey—a poignant fusion of liberation and captivity, engraved into the earth that now cradles their eternal sleep.

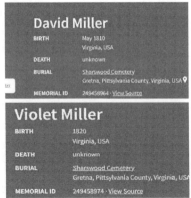

David Miller

BIRTH	May 1810
	Virginia, USA
DEATH	unknown
BURIAL	Sharswood Cemetery
	Gretna, Pittsylvania County, Virginia, USA
MEMORIAL ID	249458964 · View Source

Violet Miller

BIRTH	1820
	Virginia, USA
DEATH	unknown
BURIAL	Sharswood Cemetery
	Gretna, Pittsylvania County, Virginia, USA
MEMORIAL ID	249458974 · View Source

CHAPTER

SEVEN

Who Am I?

I spent so many years, over a decade, searching and researching the Millers and Crenshaws of Sharswood. But I am Sonya **Womack** Miranda, a woman descended from the Millers it's true, but one who bears an entirely different name. To really embrace my tree of life, I needed to embrace both sides of my family heritage. After all, there is no document or DNA evidence establishing a connection between me and the Caucasian Millers of Sharswood, only the African Millers of that plantation.

If I do not have lineage tracing back to the Caucasian Miller family, it becomes crucial to ascertain the specific origin of any Caucasian ancestry within my genetic makeup. Sarah Miller's lineage presented a formidable challenge as it reached a frustrating brick wall, with no discernible ancestors beyond David and Violet. Nevertheless, my exploration of my paternal heritage uncovered a lineage that encompassed generations of ancestors hailing from both Caucasian and African origins, the enslaved ones' history intricately intertwined with their Caucasian enslavers.

I started this journey to uncover my family tree of life at the behest of my mother and was encouraged by my cousin Alberta. I was helped along the way by stories from Dea, and with each new census and slave schedule and land deed I unlocked more about my past. Through the course of my research, I've come to a realization: the records of the enslaved were meticulously maintained. Though left off the census, slave names were primarily preserved in wills and legal documents, yet they were concealed from *us,* the enslaved and enslaved ones' decendents. It is a truth that makes it so very difficult to locate the Un-Named in one's family.

In my journey to locate Sarah and her enslaved parents, I've managed to connect the dots that lead to all of my ancestors, both enslaved and their owners. It was a pivotal moment when I stumbled upon the 1850 federal census "slave schedule," which unveiled the now-famous Violet Miller of the Sharswood plantation. This record revealed that she was born in 1822, was 28 years old in 1850, resided in the northern district of Pittsylvania County, and was owned by none other than Nathaniel Crenshew Miller.

Sharswood slave cabin

Photo by Sonya Womack Miranda

After Fred acquired the plantation, I visited it and stood at the very cabin where my ancestors once dwelled. I reached out to touch its walls, as if to communicate with their spirits, a silent gesture to let them know of me and to feel the enduring spirit that lingered there. These walls bear witness to the history that unfolded within them.

It's essential to recognize that my ancestors' history is intricately woven into the fabric of both these places, Halifax County, Virginia, and Gretna, Virginia, where they found themselves, endured, and persevered. This was Sarah's home, the place where David and Violet raised her and her siblings. And though I still didn't know the rest of Sarah's Un-Named ancestors beyond David and Violet, at least I had found some of them.

After confirming that I had no historical records or DNA connections linking me to the Caucasian Millers of Sharswood, I was driven to explore the origins of my Caucasian DNA. Interestingly, I discovered that my Caucasian lineage is intimately intertwined with my paternal family line, tracing back to my father, William Womack, Jr., and his father, William H. Womack. This lineage also extends to my paternal grandmother, Frances Luck Womack, and even further back to my third great-grandmother, Margaret Nunnally Womack, a slave born on the Nunnally plantation in Halifax County, Virginia in 1842.

Sarah's house post slavery. The slave cabins at Sharswood.

Photo by Sonya Womack Miranda

Martha Ann Womack-Ragsdale with her great nieces, my daughter Zoe and my niece Skylar. One "clue", (Nunally) given to me by Aunt Martha Ann, revealed an amazing Womack family history.

Martha Ann Womack Ragsdale, the Historian

My journey to unearth this connection began with the valuable insights generously shared by my aunt, Martha Ann Womack Ragsdale. Named after my second great-grandmother on the Luck side, Martha Ann is my father's sister. She had remarkable African features, being tall, slender, and towering at approximately 6 feet in height, a characteristic shared by many in the Womack family. Her skin was a beautiful ebony smooth color, and she had wonderfully soft, ebony hair. Prior to this, I had mistakenly believed that my father's lineage was a mix of Native American and African American ancestry, but a DNA analysis effectively corrected this misconception.

I distinctly recall an unplanned visit to my aunt Martha's home one sunny afternoon. Upon my arrival, I discovered her and her husband relishing a leisurely day. Aunt Martha was celebrated for her extraordinary culinary talents, and on that day, the delightful scent of her fried chicken permeated every corner of the house. While my main purpose was to delve into our family history, I was acutely aware of the importance of approaching these seasoned elders with the utmost care and strategy when seeking information. In their presence, one had to patiently await their moments of generosity, seizing the opportunity when they were inclined to share.

It was on this specific day that Martha Ann was more than willing to divulge family history. She shared invaluable oral family history, complemented by precious images of my grandfather William H. Womack, my cousin Green Womack, and information on the Nunnally plantation in Halifax County, Virginia. To my astonishment, her accounts aligned perfectly with historical court, deed, and land records. What she initially shared, that our family had been enslaved on what she was told was the Nunnally plantation, contradicted our last name "Womack."

The esteemed First Lady, my cousin **Linda Davis Stephens,** a dedicated Luck family historian, engages in enlightening conversations with me about our family history. It's paramount to acknowledge that these historians hold the key to unlocking our past. Seize the opportunity to delve into their rich repository of oral family history.

William H. Womack, my grandfather and "Green Womack", my father's first cousin named off the **slave**. My father was fond of his first cousin "Green." **One name** given to me by my father allowed me to uncover an unbelievable **family history**.

Visiting the Halifax County courthouse and perusing the deeds of my great-grandfather's land uncovered a treasure trove of information. Oral family history once again gave me insight into my powerful and fierce great grand-father William G. Womack; however, it was now time to see if the information provided by his nephew Douglas Womack, my father William Womack, and my aunt Martha Ann Ragsdale Womack was indeed true.

History Links the Womacks Directly to the Slaveowner

Our family's oral history tells the story of our Womack ancestors inheriting 200 acres of land shortly after the end of slavery. This narrative sparked my curiosity because it seemed extraordinary for

Black individuals to acquire such a substantial amount of land just seven years after slavery. In my quest for answers, I delved into historical records, driven by the intriguing tales that my great-grandfather, William Green Womack, may have passed as white. I believed that this could be the source of our Caucasian ancestry and set out to find concrete evidence. To my surprise, historical documents confirmed that William did indeed inherit 200 acres of land upon his mother's death, an Un-Named former slave.

Jesse B Nunnelee
in the 1850 U.S. Federal Census - Slave Schedules

Name	Jesse B Nunnelee
Residence Date	1850
Residence Place	Southern District, Halifax, Virginia, USA
Number of Enslaved People	9
Role	Slave Owner

Margaret Nunnley's father

However, this slave, unnamed in census records, was named in the will of Jesse B. Nunnally, a Caucasian slave owner in Halifax County, Virginia. Her name was Margaret Nunnally Womack. Margaret was born into slavery in 1842 and believed to be Jesse's daughter.

It is perhaps not quite so surprising then that these 200 acres of land were bequeathed to my third great-grandmother, Margaret, in Jesse's will. The will also bequeathed his watch to Margaret's husband Green Womack, who was also a slave. Notably, Jesse's will specified the land should be given from the north side of the creek, excluding his home (Will Book 30; Page 502).

This discovery of Margaret's parentage was, without a doubt, the most astonishing revelation in all my research into my family's ancestral history. And what adds further intrigue to Margaret Womack's story is what occurred upon the death of Ellen Nunnally, Jesse's wife.

Appendix D Will and Estate Records D7, the will leaving Margaret the 200 acres of land in Halifax County Will Book 2A, pp 93-97, Will of Jesse B. Nunnaly. Transcribed by Mignon Nicholson and Mark Womack

Intersection of Two Worlds - The Slave Owner and His African Offspring

In pursuit of my ancestral heritage, a remarkable revelation emerged, blending the narratives of the Nunnally plantation and the Womack family. This narrative transcends time and brings to light the interconnected stories of two disparate worlds: that of a Caucasian slave owner and his African slave offspring.

Margaret died before acquiring the land her father left her. By the inheritance laws of the time, the land should have passed on to her son, William. However, after Ellen Nunnally passed away in 1892, a legal dispute arose. Court records detail how Jesse and Ellen's son, David R. Nunnally, and his wife refused to release the land to my great-grandfather and his siblings. In response, my great-grandfather and his siblings brought their case to court, initiating a chancery suit. My great-grandfather William and his siblings Robert Lee

Womack, John Henry Womack, Mary Ellen Womack, and Ardelia Womack sought to secure their rightful inheritance.

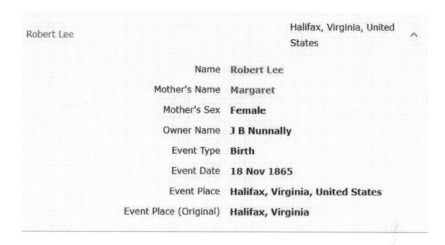

Robert Lee		Halifax, Virginia, United States	∧

Name	**Robert Lee**
Mother's Name	**Margaret**
Mother's Sex	**Female**
Owner Name	**J B Nunnally**
Event Type	**Birth**
Event Date	**18 Nov 1865**
Event Place	**Halifax, Virginia, United States**
Event Place (Original)	**Halifax, Virginia**

Robert Lee Womack would later have to sue D.R. Nunnally to get his rightful inheritance, left to his mother Margaret Nunnally Womack.

1870 United States Federal Census for Margarett Womack
Virginia > Halifax > Birch Creek

874	874	Nunally	Jesse	63	1807	Male	White	Farmer	3000	800	Virginia
874	874	Nunally	Ellen	63	1807	Female	White	Keeping House			Virginia
875	875	Womack	Green	28	1842	Male	Mulatto	Farm Laborer			Virginia
875	875	Womack	Margarett	27	1843	Female	Black	Keeping House			Virginia
875	875	Womack	Robert	3	1867	Male	Black				Virginia
875	875	Womack	William	3	1867	Male	Black				Virginia
875	875	Womack	John			Male	Black				Virginia
876	876	Nunally	John	22	1848	Male	Black	Farm Laborer			Virginia
876	876	Nunally	Francis	19	1851	Female	Black	Keeping House			Virginia

Note, Margarett's residence, in the 1870 census. She is listed as living in the residence next door to Jesse Nunally, her former slave-owner(father). In less than two years, her husband Green purchased 108 acres of land from Jesse Nunally in 1872. In this record Margaret is listed as Black. In other records she is listed as Mulatto.

The court summons to determine the legal owners of the Womack land willed to Margaret.

I was astonished to find a **black man in 1895 sued a Caucasian landowner** and **won**. The courts granted the contested land to the rightful heir. In addition to the 200 acres willed to the African Womacks, my second great-grandfather James Green Womack had purchased an adjoining 108 acres from Jesse Nunnally in 1873 for $639.43. This means they had a total of 308 acres of land. Considering that this sale took place just eight years after the Civil War and the abolition of slavery, it's remarkable this feat was achieved, and served to strengthen my belief that my Womack ancestors may have been the descendants of a slave master. The census records list all the Womacks as mulatto and oral family history has suggested that my grandfather William was well-connected.

D. R. Nunally ordered to turn land over to sheriff.

Black Landownership Post-Slavery

1865 marked the abolition of slavery with the creation of the 13th Amendment and although many people were now free, they were still being restricted in some ways. Common issues causing land loss among freed slaves and their descendants included a lack of necessary paperwork and documents. The lack of or inability to produce these items resulted in unequal access to the programs and services that would have assisted them with both obtaining land and ensuring that it remained within the family. Many newly freed slaves lacked necessary documents such as birth certificates that would prove their identity. They were able to obtain citizenship documentation after being freed, as they were required to register for citizenship, but this documentation was not seen as proof of identity, despite the fact that many freed slaves were given the same last names as their owners.

By the turn of the 20th century, former slaves and their descendants had amassed 14 million acres of land. Black agriculture was a powerhouse; per capita there were more black farmers than white farmers. But by the turn of the 21st century, 90 percent of that land was lost. Some of that can be chalked up to the Great Migration when southern blacks fled to northern cities to escape the racist violence and systemic oppression of the South. Less known is the story of those who stayed in rural areas and their efforts to hold on to their land within a legal system that seemed designed to shift it — and the generational wealth it represented — to white ownership.

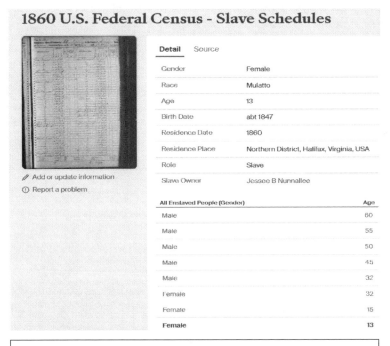

1860 U.S. Federal Census - Slave Schedules

Detail	Source
Gender	Female
Race	Mulatto
Age	13
Birth Date	abt 1847
Residence Date	1860
Residence Place	Northern District, Halifax, Virginia, USA
Role	Slave
Slave Owner	Jessee B Nunnallee

All Enslaved People (Gender)	Age
Male	60
Male	55
Male	50
Male	45
Male	32
Female	32
Female	15
Female	13

Add or update information
Report a problem

My Margaret was born in 1843. I suspect the 13-year-old female mentioned could be her. Note her race designation. Birth dates for enslaved individuals often vary. Interestingly, this record was off by four years. Jesse Nunnally owned a considerable amount of land, yet he only had nine slaves in 1860, which leads me to believe this could indeed be Margaret.

1878-042   Chancery Causes: Heirs of William W. Womack   257
Halifax County
                                        v
                              Exr of William W. Womack, etc.
                    Clardy, Powell, Vasser, White, Guthrie,
CA: Estate dispute   Pope, McDowell, Lovelace, Booth, Simms,
T: Migration   Hannah, Cofer, Hickman, Rucker,
T: Property   Stovall, Sims, Nancy~, Jacob~, Caroline~,
T: Slavery   Walter~, Cornelia~, Eliza~, Sally~,
AI: Various heirs   Lewis~, Cynda~, Solomon~, Winney~,
of William W. Womack, Silla~, Kissey~, Old Isaac~,
see Powell's affidavit, Chester~, Peter~, Lizza~,
do not reside in Va.   Nancy~, Ester~, Loretha~
Womack heirs, M.C., H.W. +
Bettie Booth, reside in
Pittsylvania Co.

Will: 1866, William W. Womack, Halifax Co.
Will: 1867, Ann J. Pope, Pittsylvania Co.

* Womack's will mentions slaves + their relationships.

In another court case, an excerpt from the court case of Captain William Watson Womack, he names a slave "Old Isaac" and he is listed as an heir. Old Iasac is listed in a will having been left to **Captain William Watson Womack's wife.** I believe old Iassc is my third great-grandfather, the father of Green Womack. I am still researching this family history.

Another issue was that many freed slaves and their earlier descendants rarely had access to legal services which meant they couldn't write wills that would correctly pass down landownership and the proper titles. If land was not explicitly passed down to a certain person or group of people, the property would go to all of the next-of-kin heirs, who would have the ability to sell their piece of land without informing the others. Fortunately for my great-grandfather William, the will of Jesse B. Nunnally explicitly listed his mother as an heir to be given 200 acres of land. What William achieved in 1892, 27 years after slavery ended, was nothing short of astonishing. Margaret's son had to go to court to assert his rightful inheritance, a testament to the complex and layered history of my family.

Margaret, the **matriarch** of my Womack family, was enslaved by Jesse B. Nunnally, underscoring the deep historical connection between our families, which I was able to find in official records. This remarkable convergence of oral and recorded history has cast a brilliant light on my heritage. It's as though a new chapter in my life has unfolded, revealing the hidden facets of my heritage. I've uncovered that I am a descendant of determined individuals, including Caucasian slave owners. Instead of feeling ashamed, I embrace this revelation, understanding it as an enduring element of the American story. My heritage forms a complex tapestry, supported by DNA analysis and extensive historical records, all tracing back to the Wimbish and Nunnally families. These two distinct lineages, intertwined with meaningful relationships with African women, have etched a lasting imprint on my ancestral legacy. It illuminates the intricate tapestry of my lineage, where white ancestors are interwoven with African ancestors.

Mary Nunley 1827-1910
4th great-grandmother
⌄
Betsey J Wilson 1848-1927
Daughter of Mary Nunley
⌄
Sarah P. Wilson 1872-1939
Daughter of Betsey J Wilson
⌄
William H. Womack Sr
Son of Sarah P. Wilson
⌄
William Womack Jr
Son of William H. Womack Sr
⌄
Sonya Womack
You are the daughter of William Womack Jr

See how Ancestry connects me to the Nunnally bloodline automatically, based on my paternal blood line.

Name:	William W Womack
Residence Date:	1850
Residence Place:	Southern District, Halifax, Virginia, USA
Number of Enslaved People:	75
Role:	Slave Owner
All Enslaved People:	1

Captain William Watson Womack, the Womack slaveowner in Halifax County. It is my belief this is the origin of my maiden name. (research pending)

The Un-Named are revealed: my fourth great-grandmother Mary, born into slavery in 1827, was enslaved on the Nunnally plantation. Mary comes through my grandfather's William H. Womack's line.

An image of the land gifted to Margaret Nunnally Womack. I was taken to the site by my cousin Richard Valon Womack and to the Womack slave burial ground. I cannot convey the emotion I felt standing on his truck looking over at the land my great grandfather fought for. Photo by Sonya Womack-Miranda

113

Green Womack, Uniquely Named

Almost all of my African American Womack family, with the exception of my father, migrated to Philadelphia, Pennsylvania over the years. Although my father briefly lived in Boston, Massachusetts, he later returned to Halifax County because he fell in love with my mother. It was my father, William Womack Jr., who offered an invaluable clue as I expanded my research into my Caucasian heritage when he mentioned a cousin named "Green."

Name	Jas. G. Womack
Gender	Male
Marital Status	Widowed
Age	39
Birth Date	1846
Birth Place	Halifax Co., VA.
Marriage Date	05 Dec 1885
Marriage Place	Halifax, Virginia
Father	Isaac
Mother	Peggy
Spouse	Charlotte Williams

My fourth great-grandfather; the "G" stands for Green. Note the birth year is wrong, but the other details are correct. He was married three times.

Such a unique name turned out to hold much significance. I discovered there was a "Green Womack" born in 1842 and who is listed as mulatto in census records; and recall that I knew William G. Womack's middle initial stood for the name "Green".

My father's cousin bore a name which was passed down through nearly every generation in my family. It's likely that my father didn't know the name's true history, nor that I would be able to use it to find more ancestors to add to my tree of life. To him, Green was simply one of his first cousins who carried on the name of our ancestors.

Surname	Given Name	Race	Gender	Age	Birth Month	Birth Year	Relation to Head of House	Marital Status	Married During Census Year	Occupation
Womack	Green	Mulatto	Male	37		Abt 1843	Self (Head)	Widower		Farmer
Womack	Robert	Mulatto	Male	15		Abt 1865	Son	Single		Student
Womack	Willy	Mulatto	Male	13		Abt 1867	Son	Single		Student
Womack	John	Mulatto	Male	10		Abt 1870	Son	Single		Student
Womack	Mary	Mulatto	Female	8		Abt 1872	Daughter	Single		

Green Womack was the name which allowed me to uncover my entire family history.

Mary Womack, born in 1872. Her father was Green Womack, a slave, born in 1842.

Epaphrod Wimbish, Slaveowner

One of the things that is fascinating about researching genealogy is that the research doesn't happen in a vacuum. While I am approaching the tree from one branch, others are reaching the same connections from a different one. The more I claimed connections within the Ancestry database, the more possible ancestors and relatives were revealed to me.

My paternal great-grandparents bore the surname "Luck" which I had difficulty tracing. But the Ancestry database showed a connection to Anthony Wimbish, and that name was very easy to find. Epaphrod Wimbish held a prominent role as a slave owner in Java, Virginia. Eppy, as he was commonly known, was married to a Caucasian woman, but he also fathered a son named Anthony through an enslaved woman, who he treated as a common law wife. Anthony is my fourth-generation mulatto grandfather. Family lore says there were two sons of Anthony, two brothers with two different surnames. One brother kept the slave master's name of Wimbish. The other brother, upon becom-

Epaphrod Y Wimbish in the •••
1850 U.S. Federal
Census - Slave
Schedules

ⓘ Compare details ⬤

Name	Epaphrod Y Wimbish
Residence Date	1850
Residence Place	Southern District, Pittsylvania, Virginia, USA
Number of Enslaved People	35
Role	Slave Owner
All Enslaved People	Name
	Epaphrod Y Wimbish

More connections from the Ancestry database

ing free, chose to shed the slave master's name and adopted the name Luck, clarifying which is why my paternal grandmother bore the surname Luck rather than Wimbish. However, there's further intrigue to this narrative, delving into the captivating reality of what truly transpired.

What truly fascinated me is how Ancestry seamlessly integrated this information into my family tree. My journey commenced with the Lucks, but over time it organically evolved, revealing the name of Eppy Wimbish as it continued to weave its way through my DNA connections.

I vividly recall discussing with my mother the remarkable findings from the DNA test I undertook on Ancestry. It instantly connected me to each of my father's ancestors, spanning both Caucasian and African American lineages. This intricate bloodline link wasn't solely the result of my efforts; rather, it unfolded through a combination of genealogical research, oral history, and cross-referencing names and identities, alongside the DNA test.

Ancestry effectively unveiled the intricate connection between my Caucasian and African American Wimbish, Luck bloodlines. This revelation further solidified my conviction that Eppy was indeed the slave owner in our family's history.

Relationship to me

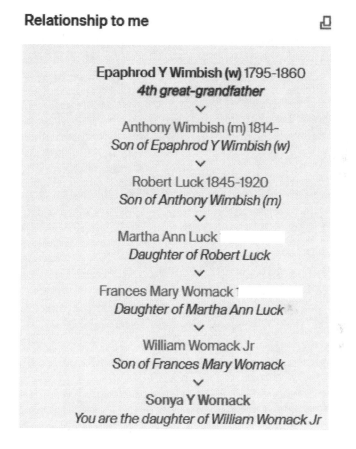

Epaphrod Y Wimbish (w) 1795-1860
4th great-grandfather

∨

Anthony Wimbish (m) 1814-
Son of Epaphrod Y Wimbish (w)

∨

Robert Luck 1845-1920
Son of Anthony Wimbish (m)

∨

Martha Ann Luck
Daughter of Robert Luck

∨

Frances Mary Womack
Daughter of Martha Ann Luck

∨

William Womack Jr
Son of Frances Mary Womack

∨

Sonya Y Womack
You are the daughter of William Womack Jr

"Unraveling the Luck Lineage to its Wimbish Roots"

Anthony Wimbish, had a son named Robert, born in 1838. Anthony was enslaved under his father Eppy Wimbish. Interestingly, Ancestry recorded Anthony's son with the surname **"Luck,"**, not **Wimbish,** a detail confirmed by official records.

It was a prevailing practice for slaves to be recorded under the names of their owners. When I searched for Robert in Ancestry, a hint emerged: the 1860 U.S. Federal Census - Slave Schedules. Upon selecting this hint, I found Robert, a twenty-year-old black male born around 1840, residing in 1860 on the JM Luck plantation. Here, the previously Un-Named Robert comes to light, shedding light on the transition from Wimbish to Luck in his name.

It appears that Robert was sold to the **JM Luck plantation**, resulting in our family surname being changed from Wimbish to Luck for him. How did I come to know Anthony's name, his father's name, and his son's name? This knowledge originates from Ancestry's tracing of our enslaved familial lineage, unraveling the mystery behind why one branch of my father's family changed their surname from Wimbish to Luck. Initially, I possessed the names of my great-grandparents, and Ancestry facilitated the linkage to their parents, which directly corroborated oral family history.

However, Ancestry's exploration delved deeper by revealing not only the slave master's name but also his son, a mulatto slave, and the son of the enslaved individual who was subsequently sold to another plantation. Once again, the "Un-Named" were identified by name in historical records, notably within the 1860 slave schedule. Within my father's family, there is a longstanding tradition of commemorating our heritage through the Luck-Wimbish family reunion.

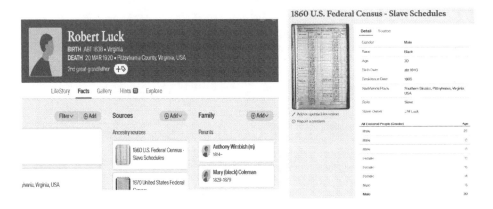

Upon adding Robert to my family tree, Ancestry seamlessly took the reins, guiding me through the intricate web of our shared past. It graciously offered clues, leading me to the invaluable resource of the 1860 slave schedule housed within the National Archives. With a single click, there he stood: my twenty-year old great-grandfather, entrenched in the confines of the JM Luck plantation. Ancestry's revelations pierced through the veil of time, unveiling Robert in the 1860 slave schedule—a pivotal moment that led me directly to my enigmatic ancestor, shrouded in anonymity. Through this discovery, I uncovered the grim truth: Robert was sold by his own grandfather, **Eppy Wimbish**, to the **JM Luck** plantation in Pittsylvania County, Virginia. The weight of this revelation lingers as I contemplate the unfathomable act of a slave owner parting with his own grandson. In my view this was a deliberate attempt to sever Robert Wimbish Luck from his familial roots and heritage. By doing so, he sought to condemn Robert to a life devoid of connection to his history, family, and identity, effectively consigning him to the ranks of the **"Un- Named."** Despite the heart-wrenching separation from his father Anthony and mother Mary, Robert endured until their long-awaited freedom arrived in 1865. His journey culminated in his passing in 1920, finding his final rest at Shokoe Baptist Church in Java, Virginia, marked by a solemn tombstone.

Here, Robert is the 20-year-old Black male.

"Breaking Chains: Their Sacrifice for Freedom"

Oral family history recounts the mysterious disappearance of a great-grandmother, sparking my quest to uncover her identity after my cousin Linda entrusted me with the task. Through diligent research, I entered my paternal grandmother's name (Luck) into Ancestry. Within seconds, two names were revealed and connected to my family tree. This journey led to the emergence of William and Sally Adams-Luck, distinctly named in the Ancestry database. Following this lead, I traced William, listed as a slave. Ancestry.com pro-

vided a straightforward path to uncover more information about William with a simple click on his name, revealing a wealth of hints, including the 1860 slave schedules. By selecting William, the platform seamlessly guided me to his slave owner, identified as JM Luck. This breakthrough opened up a significant avenue for further exploration into their histories and connections. Interestingly, this is the same JM Luck who enslaved Robert Wimbish Luck. However, there was something remarkable about Sally's husband, William, that explained Sally's disappearance.

Chains of Courage: A Fugitive's Journey to Freedom

The revelations unearthed from the 1860 slave schedules hit me like a tidal wave, exposing the raw truth about my ancestor, William Luck. The mere mention of his name, documented as a fugitive from the JM Luck plantation, sent shivers down my spine. At just twenty-five years old, he made a decision that would alter the course of his life forever—he chose to break free from the shackles of slavery and embrace the unknown path to liberty. As I reflect on William's courageous act, I couldn't help but imagine the fierce determination that must have coursed through his veins, driving him to defy the oppressive chains that bound him. And in his brave escape was the key to unraveling the mystery surrounding the disappearance of his beloved first wife, Sally Adams Luck.

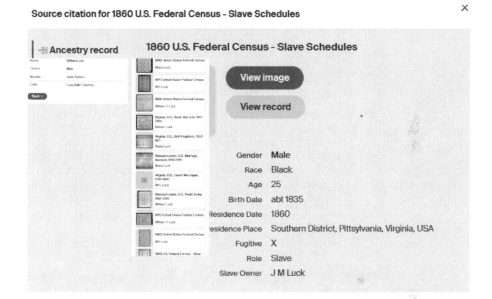

Source citation for 1860 U.S. Federal Census - Slave Schedules

As I integrated William into my family tree, Ancestry unearthed a revelation that caught me off guard. The clue lay within the 1860 census records, revealing not just one, but two great-grandfathers enslaved on the JM Luck plantation. Among them was a twenty-five-year-old black male documented as a fugitive from the plantation—my courageous great-grandfather, William W. Luck.

Their longing for freedom burned brighter than any fear of the unknown, igniting a flame of resilience that refused to be extinguished. The very thought of William's daring escape fills me with an overwhelming sense of pride and admiration. He didn't just run away; he took a leap of faith into the depths of uncertainty, guided only by the flickering beacon of hope that awaited him on the other side.

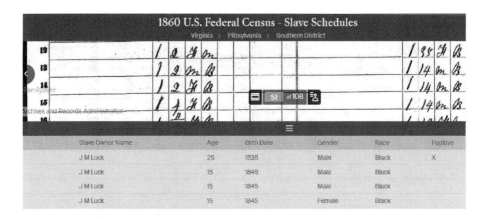

1860 U.S. Federal Census - Slave Schedules				
Virginia › Pittsylvania › Southern District				

Slave Owner Name	Age	Birth Date	Gender	Race	Fugitive
J M Luck	25	1835	Male	Black	X
J M Luck	15	1845	Male	Black	
J M Luck	15	1845	Male	Black	
J M Luck	15	1845	Female	Black	

According to historical documents, it would seem William found his way to Massachusetts . The mere mention of Massachusetts stirs my soul, a whisper of possibility that William may have found solace in its embrace. By the time the 1870 census rolled around, William and Sally had reclaimed their lives, standing tall as free individuals once more, their spirits unshackled and their hearts overflowing with gratitude. Their journey from bondage to freedom is a testament to the resilience of the human spirit and a beacon of hope for generations yet to come.

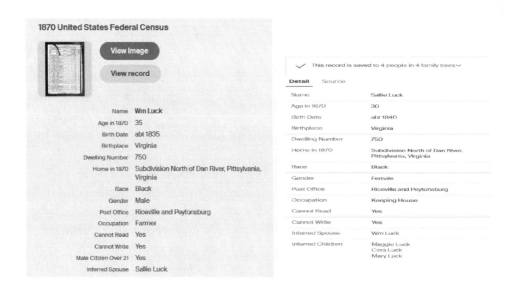

1870 United States Federal Census

View Image

View record

Name	Wm Luck
Age in 1870	35
Birth Date	abt 1835
Birthplace	Virginia
Dwelling Number	750
Home in 1870	Subdivision North of Dan River, Pittsylvania, Virginia
Race	Black
Gender	Male
Post Office	Riceville and Peytonsburg
Occupation	Farmer
Cannot Read	Yes
Cannot Write	Yes
Male Citizen Over 21	Yes
Inferred Spouse	Sallie Luck

This record is saved to 4 people in 4 family trees

Detail   Source

Name	Sallie Luck
Age in 1870	30
Birth Date	abt 1840
Birthplace	Virginia
Dwelling Number	750
Home in 1870	Subdivision North of Dan River, Pittsylvania, Virginia
Race	Black
Gender	Female
Post Office	Riceville and Peytonsburg
Occupation	Keeping House
Cannot Read	Yes
Cannot Write	Yes
Inferred Spouse	Wm Luck
Inferred Children	Maggie Luck Cora Luck Mary Luck

"Untangling Family Bloodlines"

In the depths of my family's history lies a captivating mystery, one that revolves around William and his two wives. Sallie, whom I once thought to be my great-grandmother, was merely the beginning of a tale. Little did I know, Ancestry held the key to unraveling the true identity of my great-grandmother, concealed within the whispers of DNA.

In a breathtaking twist of fate, the ancestry database unveils yet another astonishing revelation. As I delved deeper into the records, a truth emerged that left me utterly incredulous. William, my blood ancestor, stood at the heart of this newfound discovery. Yet, the image displayed before me painted a complex portrait of familial connections. There, in black and white, was Sallie, his first wife, linked to my second greatgrandfather.

But alongside her stood Sylvia, his second wife, unmistakably identified as my second great-grandmother. The distinction was clear because as it turns out Sylvia bore my great-grandfather Robert, Sallie did not. The realization struck me like a thunderbolt. In this intricate web of lineage, where bloodlines intertwine and stories intertwine, I found myself grappling with the depth of human connection. It's nothing short of miraculous how the ancestry database weaves together the threads of our DNA, illuminating the intricate tapestry of our familial heritage. As I pondered this revelation, I couldn't help but marvel at the vastness of our interconnectedness. Across generations and continents, our ancestors' lives intertwine with ours, leaving an indelible mark on our collective journey. In each discovery lies a testament to the resilience of the human spirit and the enduring power of familial bonds.

The journey of tracing our roots is a profound and deeply personal one, offering a glimpse into the lives of those who came before us. With each piece of the puzzle we uncover, we honor their legacy and pay homage to the rich tapestry of our shared history.

"Embracing My Calling to Illuminate the Un-Named"

As I poured my heart into writing this book, I couldn't help but wonder about the immense courage and strength that my ancestors, William Luck and Sally Adams Luck, must have possessed when they made the life-altering decision to run from the horrors of slavery. Imagine the turmoil they must have felt, the unbearable weight of their chains, and the relentless cruelty inflicted

Wm Luck 1835-1919
2nd great-grandfather
v
Robert Luck 1877-1950
Son of Wm Luck
v
Frances Mary Womack
Daughter of Robert Luck
v
William Womack Jr
Son of Frances Mary Womack
v
Sonya Y Womack
You are the daughter of William Womack Jr

upon them day after day. Yet, despite the risks, they chose to defy their oppressors and grasp for the elusive promise of freedom. Their decision was not just about their own liberation; it was about securing a better future for generations yet unborn, including me. They made the ultimate sacrifice, risking their lives so that their descendants, like myself, could taste the sweet nectar of liberty. Living in a time when the darkness of slavery seemed neverending, they held onto hope and determination, knowing that even if they couldn't witness it themselves, their actions would pave the way for a brighter tomorrow. I pondered whether they were acquainted with my other great-grandfather, Robert Wimbish Luck? After all they were on the same plantation. Why did Robert stay on the JM Luck plantation?

"Illuminate the UnNamed" embodies a commitment to acknowledging individuals whose stories have languished in obscurity or been disregarded, represented by the term "Un-Named." It emphasizes the significance of bringing attention to marginalized voices and their lived experiences, often within historical, societal, or personal contexts. This calling involves a steadfast dedication to advocacy, storytelling, or historical inquiry with the goal of revealing and commemorating the existence and impact of those who were never recorded as having existed in historical books."

Their courage was boundless, their sacrifice immeasurable. As I write these words, I feel their presence, their unwavering resolve echoing through the annals of history. They ran so that their son Robert, my grandmother Francis, my dad William, and ultimately, their great great-granddaughter Sonya, could breathe the air of freedom. Their legacy lives on in me, a testament to the indomitable spirit of those who dare to defy the shackles of oppression. Amen.

It is a tremendous honor to recount the stories of each member of my family. I never anticipated that delving into the search for Sarah would lead me through such diverse avenues and intertwining branches of family trees, revealing countless tales of triumph, courage, and resilience.

Family Ties in Slavery

I've connected with every branch of my ancestral tree, including the Millers, Womacks, Lucks, and Wimbishes. I've touched the walls of their existence, from the Elmina slave castles in West Africa to the slave cabins and walls of Sharswood, and even the walls of my great-great-grandmother Sarah's house in rural Pittsylvania County, Virginia. Throughout this journey, I've discovered the indomitable spirit of my enslaved ancestors who, despite the cruelty of slavery, exhibited remarkable courage and strength. I've even discovered compassionate slaveowners who developed kinships and relationships with their slaves and, though perplexing, it shows there could be some degree of humanity in something so inhumane as the system of enslavement.

My Caucasian Ancestry

The distribution of the Nunnally family evolved over time, as evident from various census records. The Nunnally family name was present in the U.S. from 1840 to 1920, with the highest concentration observed in 1880. In 1840, Virginia was the residence of 30 Nunnally families, accounting for approximately 63% of all recorded Nunnally families in the U.S. Virginia had the largest population of Nunnally families during that year. Margaret Nunnally Womack's presence is documented in the 1870 Census, where she is recorded as the wife of Green Womack, my second great-grandfather. Margaret's Nunnally lineage can be traced back to the Nunnally family, who were slave owners. I suspect that Green may also be a direct descendant of a Womack slave owner, as he is classified as "Mulatto." The close-knit relationships between the Caucasian Womacks and Caucasian Nunnally families suggest that Green may have benefited from these strong connections.

Likewise, an analysis of the movement of Wimbish families across different census years unveils a similar trend. The Wimbish family name was documented in both the U.S. and the United Kingdom between 1840 and 1920, with the most substantial presence in the U.S. occurring in 1880. In 1840, there were three Wimbish families living in Georgia, making up about 30% of all recorded Wimbish families in the U.S. In 1840, Georgia, Virginia, and South Carolina had the highest populations of Wimbish families.

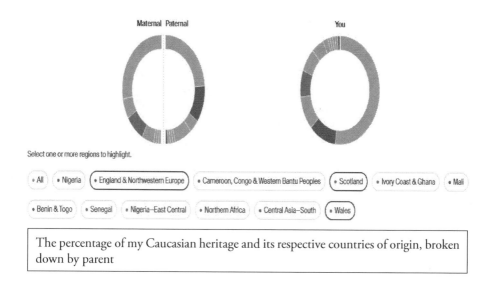

Maternal Paternal   You

Select one or more regions to highlight.

• All • Nigeria (• England & Northwestern Europe) • Cameroon, Congo & Western Bantu Peoples (• Scotland) • Ivory Coast & Ghana • Mali

• Benin & Togo • Senegal • Nigeria–East Central • Northern Africa • Central Asia–South (• Wales)

The percentage of my Caucasian heritage and its respective countries of origin, broken down by parent

My African Ancestry

As more and more people become interested in their family her-itage, technology has evolved to aid them in their quests to discover their roots. A number of commercial companies offer to test a person's DNA using genetic material gathered from a simple cheek swab that you can mail to the company's lab for testing and DNA sequencing.

After all the research I had done in the official records to prove my roots, I naturally decided to engage in the practice and see what science could tell me about my ethnic background. With DNA tests from two companies, I've solidified my African ancestry, reaching back to the early 1800s, and my Caucasian heritage, tracing as far back as the 16th to 17th centuries.

My DNA analysis confirmed that I was 54% Nigerian, of the Hausa and Fulani tribes. Knowing that, I believed my ancestors may have been brought from Nigeria to Ghana and shipped out to sea as Elmina was one of the main shipping ports and more popular slave castles in close proximity to the Nigerian coast.

The Hausa-Fulani is an ethnic designation that includes the Hausa and the Fulani tribes, ethnic groups that are spread through-

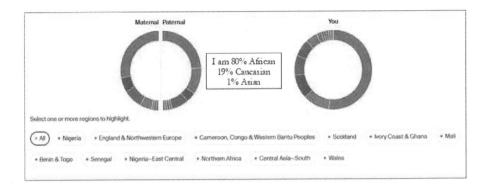

out West Africa with smaller populations in other African regions. The combined Hausa-Fulani category refers to Hausa and Fulani living in northern Nigeria. Hausa people are found chiefly in north-western Nigeria and adjacent southern Niger. They constitute the largest ethnic group in the area, which also contains another large group, the Fulani. Perhaps one-half of the Fulani are settled among the Hausa, but the Hausa are the ruling class, and those Fulani living among them have adopted the Hausa language and culture.

With the expansion of trade in the eighteenth century and the "holy wars" of Fulani in the nineteenth century, Hausa immigration to Ghana increased. Hausa traders, Muslim priests, and Hausa-speaking slaves helped to spread the Hausa culture in Ghana. Hausa tribe is Africa's largest ethnic group with 78 million people. Hausa is Africa's second most spoken local language, with 120 million speakers in Nigeria, Niger, Chad, Benin, Cameroon, Togo, Central African Republic, Ghana, Sudan, Eritrea, Equatorial Guinea, Gabon, Senegal, the Gambia, and worldwide.

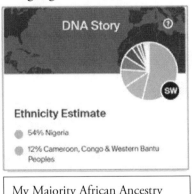

My Majority African Ancestry

128

"The Un-Named"

Captain William Watson Womack Plantation, Halifax County, Virginia,

Willam Womack Jr., bloodline (Sonya's father), research pending

1. Isaac Womack, 1800
2. Peggy Womack, 1800
3. Green Womack (m), 1842
4. Robert Lee Womack, 1865
5. Charlotte Williams Womack, 1865

Nathanie Crenshaw Miller Plantation, Pittsylvania County, Virginia

Joan Miller Womack, bloodline (Sonya's mother)

1. Rosie Miller, 1830
2. Charles Miller, 1824
3. Ned Miller, 1835
4. Margaret Miller, 1824
5. Molly Miller, 1843
6. Martha Miller, 1820
7. Charles Miller, 1856
8. Patsy Miller, 1865
9. David Miller, 1810
10. Violet Miller, 1822

JM Luck Plantation, Pittsylvania County, Virginia

Willam Womack Jr., bloodline (Sonya's father)

1. Sallie (Adams) Luck, born 1836
2. William Luck, 1840
3. Robert Wimbish Luck, 1838 (sold to JM Luck from Eppy Wimbish plantation, grandson of the slaveowner Eppy Wimbish)

4. Mary Coleman Luck, 1829
5. Lucinda Clark Luck, 1850 (originated from the Clark Plantation)
6. William W Luck, 1835
7. Sylvia W Luck, born 1847

Epaphrod Y. Wimbish Plantation, Pittsylvania County, Virginia

Willam Womack Jr., bloodline (Sonya's father)

1. Anthony Wimbish (m), 1814
2. Anthony Wimbish's mother
3. Pink Wimbish, 1858
4. Buford Wimbish, 1858
5. Charles Wimbish, 1860
6. Kate Wimbish, 1862
7. Mary Wimbish, 1834

Jesse B. Nunnally Plantation, Halifax County, Virginia

Willam Womack Jr., bloodline (Sonya's father)

1. Margaret Nunnally Womack,(m) 1843
2. Mary Nunnally, (m)1827

Unknown Plantation, research pending.

Willam Womack Jr., bloodline (Sonya's father)

1. Betsy Wilson, 1848
2. Frank Wilson, 1845
3. Matthew Wilson, 1846
4. Timothy Coleman, 1820
5. Bill Coleman, 1864

6. William T. Coleman, 1857
7. Patti Coleman, 1862

Colonel William Howson Clark Plantation, born 1780. Halifax County, Virginia 63 Slaves

Willam Womack Jr., bloodline (Sonya's father)

1. Abraham Clark (m), 1814 3rd great-grandfather, married Lucinda Luck from the Luck plantation (son of Colonel William Howson Clark), recorded in the United States Census.
2. Martha Clark, 1840
3. Sally Ann Clark, 1864
4. Marshall Clark, 1862
5. William Clark

"Threads of Love and Oppression: Unraveling the Paradox of Enslavement"

In the heart of this tale lies a paradox, woven with threads of both love and oppression. Here, within the confounding history of enslavement, emerges a portrait of complexity, where the lines between master and slave blur, and the human spirit yearns for recognition. Jesse B. Nunnally's plantation holds within its soil the story of Margaret Nunnally Womack, born to Jesse B. Nunnally and nestled within the folds of her father's legacy. In her inheritance, she inherits not only land but also the weight of her lineage, a reminder of the intricate dance between power and love.

In this intricate tapestry of humanity, love and oppression converge, forging bonds that defy the boundaries of time and space. Here, amidst the harsh realities of enslavement, one finds traces of compassion, acknowledgment, and even love, reminding us that within the darkest chapters of history, the human spirit perseveres, seeking connection, recognition, and ultimately, freedom.

Note: There were more, but I chose not to list them all.

"If they had no names, how did I find them?

CHAPTER
EIGHT

Africa, the Journey Home

Last Sunrise

The day my mother Joan called me and asked, "Sonya, do you prom-
ise to find the *tree of life?*" has left an indelible mark on my life's
journey. After hanging up, I wandered around my house in a daze.
I realized that it was time for me to make a journey I had hoped to
postpone: a return to Ringgold, Virginia, to be by my mother's side.
For years, I had traveled down Highway 29 South from the greater
Washington DC area to visit my childhood home in Pittsylvania
County, Virginia, but this trip was different.

On that fateful day, September 10, 2017, I embarked on a long
and profound journey home. I packed up pictures, albums, and even
a black dress, hoping I wouldn't need it. But something deep inside
me whispered that this journey wouldn't be a short one; it was clear
that my mother's time was drawing near.

Upon my arrival that evening, I settled into my childhood bed
in Ringgold, knowing that the following morning, visiting hours
would begin at SOVAH Health Center. I arrived at SOVAH around
6 am, and as I stood by my mother's bedside on that poignant morning, we engaged in a conversation. She was still in good spirits and
of sound mind, but the weariness of battling illness and countless
hospital visits had taken its toll. This time, when the doctors deliv-
ered the grim prognosis, she agreed with them. She turned to me and
asked if it was acceptable for her to let go.

Only 18 months prior, my sister Stephanie had passed away, a
loss that had deeply shaken my mother. I had witnessed her health

deteriorate rapidly in the aftermath of Stephanie's untimely passing. On this day, the only thing weighing on her mind was the well-being of her descendants once she departed. Without hesitation, I reassured her, "Ma, you can go now," trying to hold back my tears so that her last view of me would be a joyful one. "Please, let go." No one wants to lose their parent, but witnessing her suffering had become unbearable, far worse than the impending loss.

The first time I'd stood by Joan's bedside in a hospital my daughter Zoe had been a four-year-old; now, the last time I would be at my mother's side, Zoe was fifteen. My prayers had shifted. I no longer prayed for her to stay for the sake of Zoe who had spent countless holidays with her grandmother and summers learning to fish with her. Now, I simply wished for my mother's pain to end. Now, at the end, I recalled how my mother and I had dreamed of taking a family trip to Africa to reconnect with our roots, but circumstances prevented us from realizing that dream.

On her final day, I secretly recorded a conversation with my mother, knowing that she would have objected if she knew I was recording. I wanted to capture her voice, her last words to me, and her presence on her final day in this life. She shared how proud she was of me, her best daughter, and how I had made her proud throughout my life. Despite my efforts to remain strong, I couldn't help but sob. I reciprocated her sentiments, telling her that she had been the best mother and role model anyone could ask for. My mother's parting words included a request that I continue searching for our family's "tree of life." She was in good spirits and resolute, knowing it was time to join my father William, my grandfather Charlie, Anglean, Sarah, David, Violet, Rosie, Charles, and a host of other ancestors who had already passed on.

And so on September 11, 2017, at 10:13 am, I stood by her bed as Joan Miller Womack took her last breath and rejoined our ancestors.

With her passing, the most cherished leaf on Sarah Miller's tree of life fell. But she left me enriched with our culture, history, ancestral roots, images of our forebears, and the stories that would keep me connected to them long after her departure. Unlike many, I am fortunate to have immediate relatives who shared our family's history beyond just our grandparents. My mother and her father ensured that I was well-equipped to know my family roots, a gift I treasure deeply.

After my mother's death and funeral, I returned home, but came back to Ringgold that winter. My mother had always depended on me for everything, even on her deathbed, confirming that I had the deed to her house, paid the taxes, and possessed a copy of her will. I had assured her that her home was secure and would be passed down to her grandchildren, fulfilling her wish that it remains in our family for generations to come. It was challenging to visit that place without her presence to light up the rooms, and I couldn't bring myself to stay in her house for some time. Instead, when I came to Ringgold to engage in family research, I chose to stay with my aunt Althea.

With my mother gone, my dedication to my research deepened. I was on a quest to delve into the Miller family history, driven by a desire to honor the woman who had initiated this journey. I didn't consult any literature or genealogists on tracing enslaved ancestors; instead, I followed my instincts, guided by an inner voice urging me forward.

Fulfilling Promises

I was now in the phase of my research where I sought to uncover the stories of the unnamed slaves. My journey to Africa became a pressing need, a need to pilgrimage to the land from which my ancestors were torn away. But Africa is a large continent, and I needed to narrow my focus, to find the country and culture to which I belonged. I prepared by having my DNA tested, receiving results from two different companies. The moment those results arrived, I was filled with excitement, knowing they held the key to connecting with my motherland; the revelation would finally free me from the burden of not knowing my origins. And when I discovered my DNA connected me to the Hausa-Fulani ethnic group, I made plans to visit Ghana.

I turned 50 in 2018, a milestone year in my life. It seemed fitting to celebrate my birthday in a huge way. This was going to be both a celebration and a journey to my ancestors' homeland. My husband, Esmond, agreed that this was precisely what I needed, considering the emotional toll of the previous two years. I decided to extend my trip to explore the motherland. I planned an 11-day trip. I was ready for the profound journey that awaited me, one that would lead me to my roots, to the Middle Passage, and to the heart of my ancestral history. My primary goal was to be adopted by my tribe, the Hausa.

I discovered a group of women in Howard County, Maryland, who were planning a trip to Africa in September of 2018. It felt like destiny had aligned the stars, presenting the perfect timing for this journey. Leaving my daughter and husband behind, I embarked on a voyage of

Dr. Vanessa, Rebecca, me, Chris and Meshawn in the back. "The Ghana Sistas"

restoration and rejuvenation, ultimately seeking a profound connection with my ancestral homeland. Upon receiving my visa, I fulfilled a long-standing promise to myself and my family. Together with my newfound companions – Rebecca, Meshawn, Dr. Vanessa, and Chris – I boarded a Delta Flight at Dulles Airport, bound for Accra, Ghana. These remarkable women, whom I will cherish for a lifetime, became my Ghana sisters. It was Rebecca who had organized the trip and emerged as an extraordinary and inspiring individual. Her tireless efforts included significant contributions to building schools and libraries in Ghana.

I had extensively studied the history of the Gold Coast, as it was formerly known, prior to setting foot on its soil. As I disembarked from the plane in Accra, Ghana, I was warmly greeted by a fellow African who welcomed me. In response to his inquiry about my origin, I initially replied, "I am from the United States." However, upon closer examination, he asserted, "No, you are from Africa. What took you so long to come home?" His words struck a chord deep within me, and tears welled up in my eyes. For the first time, I truly realized the profound connection I had to this land. During a stop in Accra, I disembarked from the van, found a patch of soil, and removed my shoes to plant my feet firmly on African ground. Goosebumps covered my body, and I whispered, "Indeed, I am home."

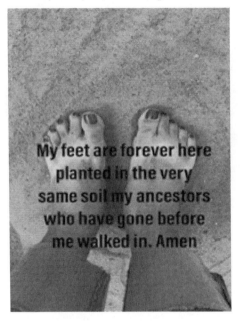

I yearned to walk on the same soil that my ancestors had trod centuries ago, and now, I had fulfilled that desire. My guide shared the rich cultural traditions of Africans with me. He emphasized the significance of elders within the family, the bearers of ancestral history, passing down stories from generation to generation by the light of the moon and a crackling fire in the evening breeze. These elders ensured that the names of great-grandparents, who had toiled tirelessly to provide for their descendants, were known to each generation.

"They made their children know the names of their great-grandparents who had toiled hard to give them survival and a home. The disconnection between pasts and your roots started with slavery. But thanks to technology, you can find your ancestors simply by doing your due diligence. You have to speak to the elders in your family before they pass away, ma'am", he said. "Some will talk to you and a lot of them will not. Be prepared for the second brick wall. There are family members who will tell you to let sleeping dogs lie, and to stop shaking the tree. The older generations seem to still be stuck in time. Do not be discouraged, find someone who is willing to share your ancestral history." His words rang true, and I vowed I would not give up my search for the Un-Named once I returned home, no matter the difficulties.

We embarked on a long journey from Accra to the central region of Ghana, visiting Cape Coast and Elmina. As we entered the renowned El Mina slave castle, my thoughts were consumed by the profound realization that this was the ultimate and final stop for my ancestors. It marked the concluding chapter of their experiences in their homeland before embarking on the perilous voyage across the ocean, shrouded in uncertainty about their destination. Tragically, some of them never reached the shores they hoped for; they perished during the grueling journey.

My feet on the floors of the slave castle.

Every moment spent on the castle's floor signified that they had bid a somber farewell to the freedom they once cherished, with the grim awareness that they might never savor it again in their lifetime.

The portal to the slave ships.

Standing motionless within the castle, I gazed through a gate towards the vast expanse of the Atlantic Ocean, attempting to fathom the experience of my unnamed ancestors.

During our visit to Elmina Castle, I had an unforgettable experience. The guide led me to the dungeons where slaves were held before being transported to Europe or the Americas. Upon entering, tears welled up in my eyes, and I began to feel an inexplicable coldness, particularly in one area of the dungeon. I shared my feelings with the guide, who acknowledged that many African Americans reported similar experiences. I was convinced that I was standing where my ancestors had been held before their harrowing journey to America.

Here was where the enslaved had waited, for months at a time, bracing themselves for the impending journey out to sea. If a female became pregnant by a slave-trader, her life and the life of her baby were spared as they would remain in the slave castles as servants instead of being shipped out to sea. The lingering smell of human suffering within the castle walls served as a stark reminder of the inhumane treatment that has scarred humanity's history. It is an odor that will forever haunt my memories.

I felt a profound connection to my African ancestors during this emotional and awe-inspiring experience. I reached out to touch the walls that had witnessed their departure, their powerlessness against the force of the Great Hurricane. Determined to understand their experience, I asked the guide to describe the procedure slaves underwent as they boarded the ships.

I felt an irresistible urge to pass through the very portal through which these enslaved individuals were lowered into boats, transformed into cargo on colossal slaving vessels, drifting farther away from their homeland, their last glimpse of freedom forever relegated to the past. I needed to do this to gain an understanding of the unimaginable trials endured by my unnamed ancestors, my Womack and Miller forebears. Somehow, against all odds, they had endured the treacherous Transatlantic slave voyage and the harrowing Middle Passage. Today, I stand as a testament to their indomitable spirit, resolute in my determination to share their remarkable story.

Touching the Walls. These walls bore witness to my ancestors' final moments on African soil. Perhaps they touched the same wall as they exited the dungeon.

When we reached the seashore, my tears flowed uncontrollably, and I shivered in the strong wind. My feet felt unsteady on the same ground where my ancestors were cast adrift. I needed to feel the same pain they had felt as they gazed back at their homeland, knowing they would never return. It was a deeply spiritual encounter, and I felt the connection within my spirit and soul. Stepping further into the sea, I shouted, "I will meet you again." The words flowed from me without conscious thought, marking the spiritual essence of my experience at Elmina Castle.

Final Sunset

My DNA test results had confirmed my African ancestry's country of origin as Nigeria. Nigeria played a significant role in the transatlantic slave trade, with over 3.5 million slaves being shipped from its coast to the Americas. The majority of these slaves were Igbo and Yoruba, with notable numbers from Hausa, Ibibio, and other ethnic groups. My initial purpose for visiting Africa was to be adopted by my Hausa tribe, a plan I had shared with the elders in Africa. However, during my journey, I felt a compelling urge to undertake an unexpected mission not initially on my radar.

Saying goodbye to my mother had not been easy, but it was during my trip to Africa that I found peace with her passing. On September 23, 2018, around 7:29 p.m., I stood on the African coast near Elmina Castle, the infamous location from which my mother's ancestors had been cast out to sea. It had been approximately one year since my mother's passing. In the darkness, I stood alone with my thoughts, holding my mother's obituary in my hand. I had mourned her and my sister for over a year, and now, I was ready to release my anger, grief, and sorrow.

If you were told that once, you cross a door you wouldn't be able to return home ever again? Would you cross it? For 12 million slaves that we know of this wasn't a choice but a real experience in history.

This was my second sunset ceremony, a year after my mother's passing. I sent her on a journey across the same waters where her ancestors had been sent across the Atlantic to the Americas. But this time, she was being returned to her homeland, Mother Africa.

To this day, I cannot explain why I had carried my mother's obituary to Africa, but as I stood by the water's edge, I intuitively knew it was the right time. I released my mother's obituary into the water, watching it float away. I whispered to her, "After today, I will no longer grieve for you. I am returning you to your ancestors, a homecoming that many of them never had the chance to experience." And just like that, my mother's memory sailed out to sea, reuniting her with David, Violet, Ned, Mollie, Margaret Miller, Moses, Peggy, old Isaac, Sally, Robert, Green, Margaret Nunley Womack, and countless other enslaved ancestors.

Later, I shared the poignant narrative of how I had symbolically cast my mother's obituary adrift at sea to the pastor of the Ghanaian church where I was to celebrate the Feast of Tabernacles. In my mind, I had braced myself for his response. To my surprise, his reaction was complementary. He exclaimed, "Wow, I understand. Your ceremony was a symbol of returning your mother to her ancestors." I was elated that he comprehended the significance of my gesture, and I wholeheartedly affirmed, "Yes indeed, that's precisely what it represented."

What Africa Gave Me

What my journey to Africa gave me in terms of closure and peace regarding my ancestors, I will never forget. But apart from being a journey of loss and sorrow, it was also a journey of hope and joy. I had come to Africa with a group of women, and then connected with members of my international church to attend the "Feast of Tabernacle". This is a fall festival that I attend every year in different parts of the world and on this momentous year I chose to celebrate in Ghana.

I had embarked on a mission to Africa with the goal of becoming an official member of my tribe, the "Hausau." I had communicated my desire to my pastor, who intended to discuss it with the village elders. However, an unexpected turn of events disrupted my initial plans.

As I became fully immersed in the African experience, meeting the local people and their children, a transformation took place within me. My focus shifted from my personal aspiration of tribal adoption to a deep commitment to giving back to my mother continent. The journey no longer revolved around my desire to be adopted by my tribe; instead, I wholeheartedly devoted myself to addressing the needs of the people I had come to know and care for.

My new family in West Africa, Kumasi, Ghana

Augustus Finn is the one wearing white. I maintain regular contact with Finn, who now serves as my social media manager.

Participating in the Feast of Tabernacles with my newfound Ghanaian church family in Kumasi, Ghana, held a special place in my heart as a cherished week. Every year, my mother and I would embark on this pilgrimage together. However, in 2018, I embarked on a distinct solo journey.

Albert, my African brother, made an enormous contribution to this book. He conducted extensive research, provided valuable insights on the African male perspective of the slave trade, and played a significant role in shaping the Transatlantic slave chapter. His writing skills are truly exceptional.

During my travels in Africa, I had the delightful opportunity to meet some wonderful individuals. Sam, the person dressed in yellow, is one of them, and we continue to stay in touch.

One of my favorite little lady bugs "Blessing". She stole my heart in Africa. I have watched her grow up since 2018.

A little lady I met in Kumasi and fell instantly in love with. The power of visiting your homeland is an experience I will never forget. Adinkra cloth is also distinguished from kente (where patterns are woven) in that its patterns are stamped on the cloth. Adinkra cloth gets its name from adinkra symbols, which convey values, such as wisdom and unity held by the Asante people. In this photo, I am making my own Adinkra cloth.

I travelled to a Ghanian fish market. I wanted to see and experience the true people of Africa.

At the Ghanaian fish market, I encountered sisters I had never met before. Among them, there was a lady wearing a scarf who initially hesitated to shake my hand because of the fish residue on her fingers. I reassured her that the scent of fish didn't bother me, as she was my African sister. With my words, she granted me permission to touch her hand. I had traveled a long way to see, feel, and connect with my people, and the fish smell was a small price to pay for the bond we shared.

The Kente cloth was crafted in Ghana, where it's traditionally women who aren't permitted to create this "sacred" fabric. However, I had the distinct honor of sitting down with a gentleman who graciously allowed me to assist him in weaving one, a moment that deeply touched my heart.

What I Gave Back

A profound desire to leave a lasting impact on the African continent, which I hold dear as my home, served as the driving force

behind my actions. This motivation was deeply rooted in my mother's heritage and, within a broader historical context, in the stories of my second great-grandmothers, Sarah and Violet, who endured enslavement in Africa. It was a moment of immense inspiration that sparked the vision of creating a program to support students in Kumasi, Ghana.

During my time in Kumasi, I had the privilege of meeting an impassioned teacher named Daniel Botha. Every day, he generously provided transportation to and from my destinations, all the while sharing his unwavering

One of my "Ghana sistas" enjoying a visit to a school where we met so many children filled with so much life.

dedication to teaching and his affection for his students. Unbeknownst to him, I was actively seeking a way to give back, and Daniel unwittingly provided the perfect opportunity.

On my final day in Ghana, I found myself with unused funds that my husband had earmarked for trip expenses. Instead of taking this money back with me, I made a conscious decision to allocate it to support Daniel's school. This choice was driven by the impact of his heartfelt commitment to his students and the noble cause of education.

Upon my return home, I felt an even stronger connection to Africa, guided by the spirit of my mother who had inspired me to explore our family's history and delve into the origins of our enslaved and African heritage. In her honor, I resolved to take even more meaningful action.

I shared my plan with my daughter, explaining that I had encountered schools in Africa facing dire needs, with students lacking essential resources such as books and desks. This inspired us to launch a fundraising initiative with the goal of making a significant impact. Additionally, we aimed to provide laptops to enhance access to technology for both teachers and students.

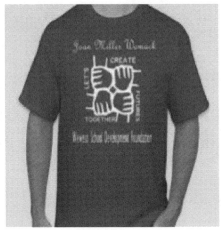

My daughter Zoe and I raised money to donate, desks, books, school supplies, tables for students who were sitting on dirt floors. Zoe was a busy honor roll student at Hammond High in Columbia, Maryland. She played varsity volleyball and club volleyball but took the time to raise money for the Weweso Schools in Kumasi, Ghana her junior year.

Taking a step forward, I initiated the creation of the Joan B. Miller Womack Weweso School Development Foundation. I reached out to friends, family, and church members to rally support for this cause. This moment marked the beginning of my transformative journey. In just a few short months, we managed to raise approximately over $5,000, contributing to a brighter future for the students and educators in Kumasi, Ghana.

I loved the children and their joy. Just seemed amazing to me how people who had so little seem to be so happy. I was inspired to do more in my mother's name. Instead of grieving I used my energy to *improve the education of children* I met while visiting.

I felt deeply honored when they included my name on one of the school buildings in Kumasi, Ghana. It was a dream that had finally come to fruition, and it meant a great deal to me. This gesture was a heartfelt tribute to the ancestors who had paved the way before me, a legacy inspired by the remarkable Sarah Miller and my beloved mother, Joan Miller Womack.

Books that the children received from our foundation. We also donated laptops and Chromebooks.

Why I felt compelled to raise money for the schools.

More books and school supplies were donated.

Image of the school we adopted. The school had over 800 students. I have found anyone can make an impact. It does not matter how big or small.

The school decided to put my name on a building after receiving the books and desks.

Desks we purchased from donations from friends, family, and church.

I witnessed the unwavering thirst for education in children who were so eager that they sat on the floor to learn. In that moment, the voices of Grandma Sarah Miller, my mother, and all my ancestors spoke to me. I realized that my mission went beyond being adopted by my tribe; I had a more profound purpose on the African continent. I left behind an indelible mark that will forever be remembered. I left the legacy of the Miller name.

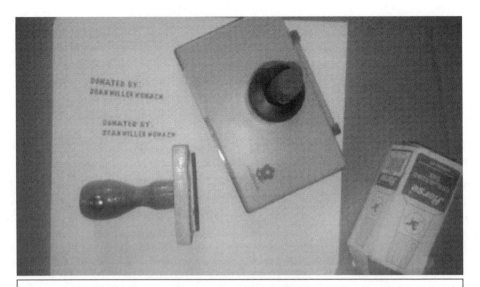

A stamp being used to tag anything donated by my mother Joan B. Miller Womack.

Sarah D. Miller and Joan Miller Womack, I believe, would be proud. They also stamped our names on any furniture we donated.

Through the grace of God and great friends, they are no longer sitting on the floor.

"Africa's Restorative Embrace: A Journey of Healing"

Alkebulan is the ancient name of Africa

It's meaning:

THE MOTHER OF MANKIND, THE GARDEN OF EDEN.

In the culmination of my quest to uncover my roots and journey to Alkebulan, I found myself deeply altered. As an African American delving into the annals of our ancestral past, I confronted the stark reality of our collective history: the relentless plundering of our freedoms, identities, and cultures by colonizers spanning the globe. It was an odyssey that laid bare the festering wounds of generational trauma, leaving me emotionally fragmented.

Yet, amidst the anguish and turmoil, my pilgrimage to Alkebulan bestowed upon me a revelation of immense magnitude. Reconnecting with the soil of my forebears, I unearthed a reservoir of resilience and faith that transcended the ravages of centuries-long oppression. Despite enduring dehumanization, my ancestors clung steadfastly to the belief that their descendants would one day reclaim their dignity and unearth the truths of our shared legacy.

In the concluding chapters of my journey, I found myself gaining a newfound reverence for my ancestors by amplifying their **silenced voices** from the era of slavery. Through meticulous research and storytelling, I honored their struggles, preserving their narratives for future generations. It dawned on me that our history isn't merely what has been handed down to us, but a tapestry waiting to be woven from the threads of our own discoveries and reflections. Indeed, the key to unlocking our past and shaping our future lies within our own hands.

Stepping foot on African soil, I grappled with a sense of disconnection from my lineage, buffeted by the echoes of a past I scarcely comprehended. Yet, as I bid farewell to the land of my ancestors, I carried with me a revitalized sense of purpose and **healing**. Through my journey, I emerged as a conduit for the silenced voices of those ensnared in the horrors of the transatlantic slave trade.

Upon returning to Alkebulan, I reclaimed not only a fragment of my identity but also sought to resurrect the legacy systematically effaced by oppression. By shedding light on their stories, I endeavored to ensure that they would never again fade into obscurity as the **"Un-Named."**

Daniel and I collaborated to commission a Ghanaian carpenter to create desks for several schools. This endeavor was my means of expressing gratitude to a country that had enriched my life in countless ways. My perspective on life underwent a profound transformation following my visit to Africa. Sarah D. Miller, Joan Miller Womack, and Charlie M. Miller inspired me and instilled the courage to continue my efforts and do even more.

EPILOGUE

My search for Sarah took over a decade. It took me through records and archives, conversations, and memories, from Virginia to Africa. I uncovered connections I never thought to find, and secrets I thought would remain hidden.

In my search to find Sarah, I found so much more than simply one woman. I discovered a generation of Un-Named ancestors, once hidden from me, but now proudly known. I learned how to be a detective, piecing together clues from records which didn't want to yield their mysteries. Each ancestor I found had been meticulously recorded in historical documents. It was through the careful preservation of these records and the passing down of their stories, their names through oral family history that I unearthed their identities.

You too can unearth your ancestors. They patiently await your recognition, longing for you to acknowledge their existence. They stand ready for you to share their tales of resilience, eager for you to inspire the next generation with the enduring legacy they have left behind. You need not remain disconnected from your past any longer. You can be whole, for you possess an undiscovered legacy that has the power to define, shape, mold, and empower you.

Begin the journey, gather the clues, and start your search. But there is a sense of urgency required. Now is the time to take action, as those precious oral historians are departing from this world, taking with them the invaluable information required to bridge the gap in your heritage.

It feels like this journey has unveiled a series of books, each unraveling the poignant story of African American slavery and the interconnected heritages within this nation. My research has now come full circle. As an African American, I've had a unique experience that few can claim to have undergone. I've physically connected with the walls of the slave cabin where David and Violet once resided, the very place where my second great-grandmother, Sarah Miller, was born in 1868. I've felt the souls of my ancestors within the slave castles in Africa and touched the walls where they were pushed towards an unforgiving sea. I've traced the footsteps of my ancestors across two continents. I no longer sense a disconnection from my heritage, my history, or my roots as an African American. I've established a tangible link to my ancestors, those who were obscured from my view. The discovery of my ancestors brings a sense of completeness, and I now feel like a whole human being, truly knowing who I am.

If you don't tell the stories, the history dies with you.

Sonya Womack-Miranda

BIBLIOGRAPHY

Ancestry. n.d. *Nunally Family History.* https://www.ancestry.com/
name-origin?surname=nunally.

—. n.d. *Wimbish Family History.* https://www.ancestry.com/name-
origin?surname=wimbish.

Apenkro, Sophia Celestina. 2023. *History of the Hausa People.* July 05.
https://www.sophiaapenkro.com/history-of-the-hausa-people/.

Banks, William M. 1996. "Race and Responsibility in American
Life." In *Black Intellectuals.* Norton: The Washington Post.
https://www.washingtonpost.com/wp-srv/style/longterm/
books/chap1/blackintellectuals.htm.

Barth, Brian. 2019. *How Did African-American Farmers Lose 90
percent of Their Land?* August 19. https://modernfarmer.com
/2019/08/how-did-african-american-farmers-lose-90-percent-
of-their-land/.

Boundless. 2016. *Slave Codes.* November 20. https://web.archive.org
/web/20170205013548/https:/www.boundless.com/u-s-
history/textbooks/boundless-u-s-history-textbook/slavery
-in-the-antebellum-u-s-1820-1840-16/slavery-in-the-u-s-122/
slave-codes-653-10159/.

Christopher, Span M. , and Sanya N. Brenda. 2019. "Education and
the African Diaspora." *The Oxford Handbook of the History of
Education* (Oxford University Press) 402.

Cornelius, Janet Duitsman. 1991. *When I Can Read My Title Clear:
Literacy, Slavery, and Religion in the Antebellum South.* Columbia,
South Carolina: University of South Carolina Press.

C-span. 2017. *National Museum of African American History and
Culture.* February 19. https://www.c-span.org/video/?423740-1/
national-museum-african-american-history-culture.

Ellis, Nicole. 2021. *Lost Lineage: The Quest to Identify Black Americans'
Roots.* October 19. https://www.washingtonpost.com/nation
/2020/02/25/lost-lineage-quest-identify-black-americans-roots/.

Elmina Castle. n.d. *Elmina Castle.* Accessed October 16, 2018. https://elminacastle.info/index.html.

Elmina Castle, Ghana. 2009. *Elmina Castle.* January 01. Accessed October 16, 2018. http://www.ghana.photographers-resource. com/locations/Heritage/LG/Elmina_castle.htm.

Estes, Roberta. 2013. *Indians and the Census 1790-2010.* May 14. https://nativeheritageproject.com/2013/05/14/indians-and -the-census-1790-2010/.

Every Castle. n.d. *Elmina Castle - Castles, Palaces and Fortresses.* Accessed October 16, 2018. https://www.everycastle.com/ Elmina-Castle.html.

Finkelman, Paul. 2006. "From the Colonial Period to the Age of Frederick Douglass." *Encyclopedia of African American History, 1619–1895 445.*

Fitzgerald, Madelene Vaden. 1987. *Pittsylvania: Homes and People of the Past.* Virginia: Homeplace Books.

Genet, Am J Hum. 2021. *So many Nigerians: why is Nigeria overrepresented as the ancestral genetic homeland of Legacy African North Americans?* January 07. https://www.ncbi.nlm.nih.gov/pmc/ articles/PMC7820629/.

Ghana Web. 2006. *Elmina Deserves World's Attention.* January 03. https://www.ghanaweb.com/GhanaHomePage/features/ Elmina-Deserves-World-s-Attention-97017.

Global Security. n.d. *Ghana History - Early Contact.* https://www. globalsecurity.org/military/world/africa/gh-history-2.htm.

Hair, P. E. H. 1995. "Was Columbus' First Very Long Voyage a Voyage from Guinea?" *History in Africa* 22: 223-237. doi:https://doi. org/10.2307/3171915.

Hart-Davis, Adam. 2007. *History: The Definitive Visual Guide.* London: Dorling Kindersley Ltd.

Harvard Divinity School. n.d. *Hausa-Fulani.* https://rpl.hds.harvard. edu/faq/hausa-fulani.

Heim, Joe. 2022. *An old Virginia plantation, a new owner and a family legacy unveiled.* January 22. https://www.washingtonpost.com /history/2022/01/22/virginia-plantation-slavery-owners-his- tory/.

Ishmael, Mensah. 2015. "The roots tourism experience of diaspora Africans: A focus on the Cape Coast and Elmina Castles." *Journal of Heritage Tourism* 213-232. doi:doi:10.1080/1743873X.2014. 990974.

Lawrence, Arnold Walter. 1963. *Trade Castles & Forts of West Africa.* London: Jonathan Cape.

Nittle, Nadra Kareem. 2020. *How the Black Codes Limited African American Progress After the Civil War.* October 01. https://www. history.com/news/black-codes-reconstruction-slavery.

PBS. n.d. *The Middle Passage c. 1600 - 1800.* https://www.pbs.org/ wgbh/aia/part1/1p277.html#:~:text=A%20slave%20who%20 tried%20to%20starve%20him%20or,a%20speculum%20 orum%2C%20which%20held%20the%20mouth%20open.

Rootsweb. 2016. *1790 U.S. Census.* October 18. https://wiki.roots-web.com/wiki/index.php/1790_U.S._Census.

Ruther, Heinz. n.d. "An African heritage database, the virtual preservation of Africa's past." *ISPRS.* https://www.isprs.org/proceedings/xxxiv/6-w6/papers/ruther.pdf.

Rüüther, Heinz , and Rahim S. Rajan. 2007. "Documenting African Sites: The Aluka Project." *Journal of the Society of Architectural Historians* 437-443. doi:DOI: 10.1525/jsah.2007.66.4.437.

Son of the South. n.d. *Illegal to Teach Slaves to Read and Write: Harper's Weekly. June 21, 1862.* http://www.sonofthesouth.net/ leefoundation/civil-war/1862/june/slaves-read-write.htm.

Span, Christopher M. 2005. "Learning in Spite of Opposition: African Americans and their History of Educational Exclusion in Antebellum America." *Counterpoints* 131: 26-53. http:// www.jstor.org/stable/42977282.

Stahl, Lesley. 2022. *How an Air Force veteran discovered his new house was the seat of a plantation where his ancestors were enslaved.* May 15. https://www.cbsnews.com/news/sharswood -air-force-veteran-plantation-ancestors-reclaiming-histo-ry-60-minutes-2022-05-15/#l38vil7fje9mk4byt3p.

The Ship List. 1977. *Settlers to Liberia* (1843-187?). https://www. theshipslist.com/ships/Arrivals/liberia.shtml.

UNESCO World Heritage Convention. n.d. *Forts and Castles, Volta, Greater Accra, Central and Western Regions.* Accessed October 18, 2018. https://whc.unesco.org/en/list/34/.

Wada, Kayomi. 2010. *EL MINA SÃO JORGE DA MINA.* January 11. https://www.blackpast.org/global-african-history/el-mina-sao -jorge-da-mina/.

Wikipedia. n.d. *Elmina Castle.* https://en.wikipedia.org/wiki/Elmina _Castle#cite_ref-Portuguese_In_WA_5-0.

Wikipedia. n.d. *1790 United States census.* https://en.wikipedia.org/ wiki/1790_United_States_census.

—. n.d. *Slavery in the United States.* https://en.wikipedia.org/wiki/ Slavery_in_the_United_States.

Williams, Heather Andrea. 2009. *African American Education in Slavery and Freedom.* Chapel Hill and London: Univ of North Carolina Press.

Zamani Project. n.d. *Elmina Castle: The first trading post built on the Gulf of Guinea.* https://zamaniproject.org/site-ghana-elmina-el mina-castle.html#header5-z.

ABOUT THE AUTHOR

Sonya has always been a free spirit who loves to travel the world. She has researched her family history for over ten years, from Virginia to Africa, in search of her roots. She believes Sarah's courage, Sarah's strength, and Sarah's will to survive were instilled in her.

Sonya's aunt Althea Gibson Miller attended Norfolk State University. After hearing Althea's story of meeting black people from the Caribbean and Africa, Sonya followed in Althea's footsteps and attended the Historically Black College as well.

Sonya holds a Bachelor's degree in Broadcasting from Norfolk State University, Norfolk, Virginia, a Master's Certification in Human Resource Management from the University of Maryland, College Park, Maryland, and a Master's Degree in Organizational Management from Ashford University, Clinton, IA. She is a member of Delta Sigma Theta Sorority Inc. Sonya holds a position as a senior-level IT training consultant.

www.unnamedsarahmiller.com

SPECIAL THANKS

Althea Gibson Miller

I want to express my deepest gratitude to my aunt Althea Gibson Miller, for her immense generosity in sharing her life with me. She wasn't just an aunt; she was a cherished friend, a supportive sister, an inspiring mentor, and an exemplary role model. Her invaluable guidance fueled the determination and passion that drove me to write this story. Furthermore, her pivotal role in bringing our family history to publication cannot be overstated. Althea's unique presence and influence will forever be irreplaceable. She loved books. Thank you, God, for blessing me with her in my life.

Sarah Brown, Editor

A heartfelt appreciation goes to the exceptional editor, Sarah Brown, who generously shared her expertise with a first-time author, guiding the process of crafting this story. Sarah breathed life into both the book and the narrative, and without her invaluable assistance, the completion of "UnNamed, the Search for Sarah Miller" would not have been possible.

Need help researching your history, contact:

Sonya Womack-Miranda at Charis Ancestry Connections
@charisancestryconnections@gmail.com

website:www.unnamedsarahmiller.com

CHARIS
PUBLISHING